Education and Deaf and Hearing Adults

A Handbook

Lesley Jones
In association with NIACE

D0490867

Withdrawn
GATESHEAD COLLEGE LEARNING CENTRES

NIACE
THE NATIONAL ORGANISATION
FOR ADULT LEARNING

Published by the National Institute of Adult Continuing
Education, 21 De Montfort Street, Leicester LE1 7GE

© 1993 NIACE

British Library Cataloguing in Publication data
A CIP record for this title is available from the British Library

ISBN 1 872941 45 1

All rights reserved. No reproduction, copy or transmission of this
publication may be made without written permission.
No part of this publication may be reproduced, copied or
transmitted, save with written permission or in accordance with
the provisions of the Copyright, Designs and Patents Act 1988,
or under the terms of any licence permitting limited copying
issued by the Copyright Licensing Agency.

This handbook is part of a two-year National Institute of Adult
Continuing Education project funded by the Joseph Rowntree
Foundation. It is accompanied by a video report in British Sign
Language produced by Lesley Jones and Gloria Pullen with Deaf
Owl Productions.

The Joseph Rowntree Foundation has supported this project as
part of its programme of research and innovative development
projects, which it hopes will be of value to policy makers and
practitioners. The facts presented and the views expressed in this
report, however, are those of the authors and not necessarily
those of the Foundation.

Printed in England by The Cromwell Press Ltd, Melksham, Wilts

Contents

GATESHEAD COLLEGE LEARNING CENTRES
371.912
JON
1006047

Foreword

This handbook is the culmination of a two-year project to highlight good practice in the field of continuing education for deaf and hard of hearing adults, undertaken by NIACE, the national organisation for adult learning, with generous support from the Joseph Rowntree Foundation. It is the second good practice guide published by NIACE, following *Adults with Learning Difficulties: Education for choice and empowerment* (1990), and NIACE is committed to produce comparable work mapping provision for adults with mental health problems and for adults with a visual impairment.

At their best, education services are alert and responsive to difference among the communities they serve. Different people have different aspirations, want or need to study in different ways and at different times, and need different practical support systems to work effectively. No single strategy works with everyone. This lesson is central to the argument of Lesley Jones' work for NIACE on education for deaf and hard of hearing adults. It has, too, been central to the process by which this book has been prepared in its final form for publication by NIACE.

We have been keen in the project to recognise that many tutors and organisers working with adult learners know little of the richness of deaf culture, or of the different practical support strategies different deaf and hard of hearing people need to be able to fully realise their aspirations as active, critical participants in learning as adults. This book is offered as a practical guide for them, drawing as it does on the richness and diversity of experience among statutory and voluntary providers, and on the experiences of deaf and hard of hearing people in organising their own learning programmes. We have not wanted to suggest that all educational providers are people without hearing problems, making provision for people with hearing impairment. We have not wanted, either, to make deaf and hard of hearing people objects of the text, with the educator as subject. We have, however, wanted to extend the range of opportunities on offer, and to challenge adult educators to extend the full riches of the education offer to deaf and hard of hearing people. As the book makes clear, there is a rich diversity of provision – you can study most things somewhere, but in too many places the diet on offer is skeletal and remedial. We have not wanted either to be insensitive to the strongly held views and values of the overlapping communities of deaf and hard of hearing people. But we do recognise that in addressing one audience you may lose the nuances of argument appropriate and relevant to others.

Any such clumsiness is wholly the responsibility of NIACE. The text has been prepared for publication by NIACE and is based on Lesley Jones' research. Credit must lie with Lesley as the key project worker. She has drawn together the fruits of thousands of people's good practice, and synthesised it into an account that will present tough challenges to everyone concerned to offer access to post-compulsory education. I am grateful to her for the generosity and imagination she has brought to the handbook and to the wider work of our project; to Gloria Pullen who has worked with Lesley on fieldwork interviews and on the video which is published at the same time as this handbook; to the steering committee for extending our vision and supporting us in realising it; and especially to the Joseph Rowntree Foundation for funding our enquiries. Many people contributed to the realisation of this project, and our thanks are due particularly to Dorothy Spence and Kaz Threlfall for administrative support. We hope and believe that this handbook will make a unique contribution to the field, and that the challenges it poses will capture the imagination of practitioners and policy-makers to work alongside deaf and hard of hearing adults to extend provision so that the best of today's practice becomes the norm by the day after tomorrow!

ALAN TUCKETT
Director, NIACE

Scope and Aims

Aims

Deaf and heard of hearing adults share with all adults an entitlement to participate in adult learning provision suited to their circumstances, needs and interests.

This handbook aims to identify the issues relating to deafness and deaf people, and to give information about ways in which adult learning opportunities can be designed to meet their needs.

The difference between people who hear and those who do not is in how they communicate. Hearing people use spoken language, whereas people who are deaf use different methods of communication, for example British Sign Language, which is a language in itself, or other methods of using spoken language such as lipreading or writing things down. The handbook describes the different languages and methods of communication which can be used and gives examples of adult learning initiatives, drawing on a survey of provision carried out by NIACE (see Appendix 1). It also identifies the practical and policy issues which arise from seeking to ensure that deaf adults have genuine access to suitable learning opportunities. In producing the handbook, the focus has been on giving essential information, suggestions for finding out more and practical guidelines to enable anyone concerned with providing adult learning opportunities to respond to the educational needs and interests of deaf and hard of hearing adults.

Who the handbook is for

The handbook is written for a number of audiences including:

- tutors in all subject areas
- deaf or special needs co-ordinators or unit staff
- managers of adult learning services or institutions
- staff development and training personnel
- policy-makers
- funding bodies
- agencies working with deaf or hard of hearing people
- anyone concerned with improving educational opportunities for deaf or hard of hearing adults, for example employers, individuals who are deaf or hard of hearing

- colleges, community education services, universities, etc., who will find the handbook useful for working with adults and with younger age-groups.

Deaf people feature not only as learners but also in all of the above categories, of course, and this is reflected in the handbook. It is written for those who are starting to learn about deafness and deaf language and culture, as well as those who are experienced and knowledgeable in this area of work.

Terminology

The term 'deaf' is used to cover all people who would describe themselves as Deaf, deafened, deaf-blind or hard of hearing, but not everyone who does not hear likes to be called deaf. In this handbook 'Deaf' with a capital D is used for Deaf people who use sign language and identify with the Deaf community. In Chapter 1 there is an explanation of different terms used for deaf and hard of hearing people, which is used elsewhere as a generic term.

Why the handbook is needed

There are some seven and a half million people in Britain who have difficulty hearing, which is around 17 per cent of the population. Hearing loss is the second most common disability. There is concern amongst adult educators at the narrow range of educational opportunities available for deaf and hard of hearing adults (mainly adult basic education, information technology, lipreading for older hard of hearing people, some communication support for people on mainstream, qualification-bearing courses and British Sign Language classes, which recruit mainly hearing people). There is also concern at the generally low participation in adult learning opportunities by people who are deaf or hard of hearing. Many deaf or hard of hearing people have had negative past experiences of schooling, and this makes adult learning opportunities particularly important as a first real chance for them to benefit from education. In addition, deaf and hard of hearing people are more likely to be unemployed or underemployed in jobs at lower levels than their abilities merit; adult learning opportunities can provide an important route into employment or promotion.

Adult educators are committed to providing learning opportunities for all adults. However, providers may be unaware of the educational needs and interests of deaf and hard of hearing adults, or they may have some awareness but are unsure of how to proceed and develop suitable educational opportunities. Thus it was felt that a practical handbook about issues and strategies for adult learning opportunities for deaf and heard of hearing people was needed to help to:

- extend the curriculum offer for deaf and hard of hearing adults
- increase the amount of provision and communication support suitable for deaf and hard of hearing adult learners
- increase the participation and successful outcomes of deaf and hard of hearing adult learners
- give providers increased knowledge and understanding of deafness and deaf and hard of hearing adults, and the kinds of educational provision they want, and the confidence to set up suitable provision.

Currently there is little else published about deaf and hard of hearing people and adult education. This kind of handbook, which aims to give an overview of the area, was identified as a much-needed resource.

Who provides educational opportunities for deaf and heard of hearing adults?

Learning opportunities for deaf and hard of hearing adults are offered, and can be developed further, across all sectors of post-16 education, as well as through voluntary organisations and employers. Examples of provision in all of these sectors are given in the handbook, which aims to encourage the development of provision across all sectors.

Legislation

The legislative base for deaf and hard of hearing adults' participation in learning opportunities through the Further and Higher Education Act rests primarily on the duty to deliver adequate or sufficient levels of provision. Definitions of 'adequate' or 'sufficient' are determined by the main funders and providers, the Further Education Funding Councils and Local Education Authorities. There have not yet been test cases of failure to provide adequate or sufficient levels of provision.

A more robust legislative framework for educational provision for deaf and hard of hearing adults is needed to strengthen and extend the level and range of provision available. Other areas of legislation can also contribute significantly to improving opportunities, for example legislation for people with disabilities.

Ways of using the handbook

The book may be read straight through, or readers may prefer to select chapters or sections they are particularly interested in, such as curriculum ideas or policy and funding issues. There are a number of good practice checklists and illustrative case studies of practice which can be used for staff discussions and for staff development and training purposes. In addition trainers may wish to create their own staff development materials drawing on the information and ideas in the handbook. The handbook can be used as background reading to guide reviews or audits of an institution's or agency's provision for deaf and hard of hearing adults, and to inform strategic and development planning exercises to improve provision for deaf and heard of hearing adults in the future.

Experiences of adults who are deaf or hard of hearing

There are descriptions of deaf and hard of hearing adult learners' views and experiences of education throughout the handbook, often giving very sharp insights into education which works and that which does not. Readers are encouraged to find out from deaf and hard of hearing adult learners, and potential adult learners what their views and experiences are of education and to involve them as far as possible in the planning and running of any provision. Often deaf and hard of hearing people's experiences as learners and teachers in education highlight very powerfully the ways in which provision falls short of what is needed, giving useful pointers to the kinds of changes needed.

> *'I went to my ante-natal relaxation class and the teacher told us to lie on the floor and close our eyes. That was it for me! I could not see her face so I could not follow after that' (a young deafened woman who had attended ante-natal classes and who is now on a childcare course).*

> *'We went on a training course from work. I'd missed a lot with everyone talking in a group, the overhead projector on and the lights out so I couldn't see the tutor's face. I asked the others afterwards but they didn't tell me everything' (a hard of hearing middle-aged working man).*

> *'The range of subjects a deaf person is allowed to follow is severely limited, not because of our ability but because further*

and continuing education organisers won't allow us to take part. I have lost count of the number of courses I've been turned down for, because tutors and organisers say, sorry we haven't got the equipment or trained people to help you take part' (a deaf adult education student).

'It was very good. I had a sign language interpreter all the time. It meant for the first time in my life I could really follow what was happening in my class, not just guessing and having to borrow notes from others' (a deaf mature student doing an A-level course).

'They (the tutors) went out of their way to be helpful, always checked that the loop was working, spoke clearly and the group did not interrupt each other' (a retired draughtsperson on a creative writing course for hard of hearing students).

The structure of the handbook

This book addresses three main issues:

- language and learning: the differences between deaf people in terms of language, communication and culture and the need for different adult learning strategies for language and communication support
- ways of working: the range of current provision
- policy, planning and participation: overall policy and planning to ensure the full participation of deaf and hard of hearing people.

1

Deafness and Difference

Deaf people, culture and identity

Deaf people are not all the same. They have different kinds of language and communication, as well as different kinds of deafness. Deaf people come from different social, economic and cultural backgrounds. Deaf people's backgrounds, as well as their deafness, significantly influence their life experiences.

Glynis is a woman in her forties, deaf from early childhood and on the Management Committee of her local Deaf club in the south-west of England. She sees herself as part of the Deaf community and uses British Sign Language. She is very active in the national Deaf Association and goes to rallies and other meetings whenever possible, fitting in with her work as a cook. She would describe herself as proud to be Deaf.

Mary is another woman of the same age, working in an office in a large Midlands town. She uses a hearing aid and relies on speech to communicate. She can manage quite well in a quiet room when she is talking to only one person, but in a crowd or a noisy pub it is difficult to hear enough to follow a conversation. Mary only began to notice the change in her hearing in her early thirties. She would describe herself reluctantly as hard of hearing if she had to describe her hearing at all.

Oswald is a man of 85 living in rural North Wales. He can no longer see the television clearly or talk to his grandchildren on the telephone. He does not hear the doorbell ring, so he often misses visitors calling on him. He would probably not describe himself as deaf or blind, although he is actually registered as being visually impaired. He sees his hearing loss as part of growing older and, like his arthritis, something he just accepts.

Sahil is 20 years old and lives in Manchester. He was deafened at the age of 15 as a result of meningitis. He is deciding whether to try and learn British Sign Language or to carry on trying to lipread or write things down. His family's first languages are Urdu and Punjabi, although the spoken language used is Urdu. This means that there are three languages which he is trying to lipread. He describes himself as deafened. He is trying to get onto a computer course at the local college.

What is deafness?

The medical definitions of deafness draw, in the main, on two ways of measuring hearing loss:

- through clinical tests which focus on measuring the decibels of hearing loss through audiological measurement
- through functional tests which focus on establishing what a person can or cannot hear in everyday contexts such as a telephone ringing or someone whispering; hearing loss is then rated on a functional scale.

Medical models of deafness tend to concentrate on the pathologising, problem-centred view of deafness, often to the exclusion of the ways in which deafness is socially constructed. Deafness is a social issue because it is an issue of two-way social communication between deaf and hearing people. Deafness means that communication between hearing and deaf people relies on different language and communication. Education can play a vital role in enabling hearing and deaf people to communicate effectively with each other, as well as supporting language learning.

The social construction of deafness can be seen in the effects of society's attitudes to and images of deafness and deaf people, which condition the life experiences and opportunities of deaf people.

Definitions of deafness

Deaf with a capital D

Deaf with a capital D is used by people whose first language is British Sign Language and who see themselves as part of the Deaf community. In British Sign Language there are different signs for people who are committed members of the Deaf community and for those who see themselves as part of the hearing world. There are about 50,000 people who use British Sign Language in the United Kingdom (about the same number as those who use Welsh). People who describe themselves as Deaf see themselves as having a language and culture of their own, quite distinct from that of hearing people. They are more likely to have been deaf from early childhood and to have been to a residential school for deaf children. This may well contribute to the strong sense of identity which many Deaf people have. The Deaf community is a distinct group in the context of and in response to the dominant hearing culture.

British Sign Language is most often learned from contemporaries in school, through school classes and through Deaf clubs, as most deaf children are born to hearing parents (about 85 per cent of deaf children have hearing parents). The way in which sign language is learned is quite different from the language acquisition of hearing children, who invariably learn their first language from parents and family.

Deaf culture relies on visual information and visual language, and involves much more touching, with eye contact and gaze as central aspects of communication. Sometimes deaf people mock the stereotype of a hearing person who is very stiff and formal and looks away nervously if anyone looks them in the eye.

Deaf people (with a small d)

The word deaf can be used generically to cover all people with different types of deafness. This includes people who are hard of hearing, deafened or deaf-blind. Some people who are deaf have been bought up and educated mainly in the hearing world and function mainly through speech, lipreading and writing using the English language (or other community languages) rather than sign language. They are sometimes referred to as oral deaf people. Some deaf adults preferring oralism who were prevented from signing in school or at home early on in life are now learning British Sign Language and want to join the Deaf community. Deafness before language development was sometimes described as 'prelingual' deafness. This term is resented now by some deaf people, who feel it is based on the

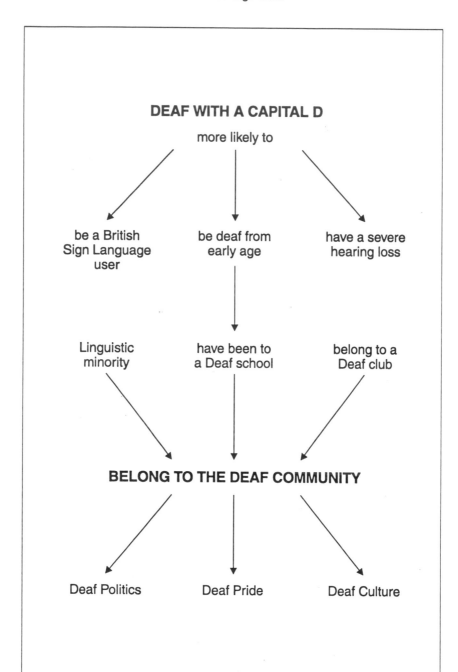

Figure 1.1 Deaf with a capital D

notion that spoken language is the only language, and it suggests that deaf people are without language, which does not give British Sign Language proper recognition.

Hard of hearing people

There are far more people who are hard of hearing than are profoundly deaf. Some 60 per cent of people over 70 have significant hearing loss. In total, around seven and a half million people have difficulties with their hearing, roughly 17 per cent of the population (Medical Research Council Institute of Hearing Research, University of Nottingham, 1988). The vast majority of these are hard of hearing.

Being hard of hearing means:

- having some hearing
- probably having a gradual, mild hearing loss
- probably being older when hearing declines (presbycusis is the medical term for a hearing loss associated with ageing)
- perhaps having tinnitus (noise in the ears, something like a jet engine or a buzzing sound)
- perhaps wearing a hearing aid (although this does not mean the person can then hear everything).

A hard of hearing person may communicate using a number of methods, including lipreading, amplification (for example a hearing aid) or reading the written word, but their communication is based on English or whatever the home spoken language is.

Being deafened

The word deafened is used to describe someone who has become pro-foundly deaf as an adult. They see themselves as different from hard of hearing people because they have no useful hearing at all, so a hearing aid is no help to them. They are different from people who have been deaf from birth or an early age or whose preferred language is British Sign Language, because their first language and the one they have used for most of their life is English or a community language.

People with acquired deafness

The term acquired deafness is sometimes used to describe hard of hearing people and deafened people. It serves to make a distinction between people who become deaf later in life and those who are born deaf.

Being partially deaf or partially hearing

These terms are not widely used. They usually refer to people who are born with partial hearing, and who may have been to a partially hearing unit in a mainstream school.

People who are hearing impaired

This term is in general use, particularly in the United States and Canada, but less often in Britain. It is seen by some people as based on a 'deficit' model of disability.

Deaf-blind people, visually and hearing impaired or people with a dual sensory disability

These terms are used for people who have both a visual and a hearing loss. This can vary in degree from totally deaf and completely blind to having some hearing and some vision. Deaf-blind people may use sign language, the manual or block alphabet; sit very close to the speaking person and listen with a hearing aid; or sit close and see signing. People with Usher's Syndrome have a tunnel of vision and can see signing close to, within a restricted visual frame.

How terms are used

Deaf people choose to describe themselves using different terms. The way in which people choose to define or describe themselves should be respected. In the past many of the words used to talk about deafness were taken from medical definitions linked either to the age of onset of deafness or to the severity of the hearing loss. The term 'Deaf and Dumb' is now generally seen as offensive, with the word dumb having connotations of intellectual impairment.

Images of deafness

There has been a controversy in the last few years over the ways in which deafness is portrayed in advertisements used to raise money by voluntary organisations. The Royal Association of the Deaf (RAD) and the Royal National Institute for Deaf People (RNID) in particular were involved in campaigns which caused complaints. An excellent discussion of the photographic portrayal of disability is found in David Hevey's book *The Creature that Time Forgot*. In this context it is interesting to look at how deafness is portrayed in society. It is particularly relevant as many people belonging to the Deaf community do not consider themselves as having a disability. There is a preference for being seen as a linguistic minority rather than as a disabled group. Hard of hearing people too are often reluctant to identify themselves as disabled, seeing themselves as part of the hearing world.

Most hearing people have heard of Evelyn Glennie or Jack Ashley, the former MP who is now in the House of Lords. These public figures can be seen as part of the 'aren't they marvellous' image of disability which some disabled people find more irritating than straightforward discrimination. It can be as much of a burden if there is a pressure to perform twice as well as someone without a disability.

A more realistic view of hearing loss is the stereotyped older hard of hearing guest, a character based on John Cleese's mother, in the television series *Fawlty Towers*. She at least fights back and makes the hearing person look foolish by controlling the conversation when the irate hotelier Basil Fawlty is failing to communicate with her. The insensitivity of his talking to her behind her back and complete failure to convey even the simplest sentences to his guest show him in a very poor light.

The American film and play *Children of a Lesser God* did a lot to publicise sign language. The performance of the play (which is performed in sign language and English) in 1986 also stimulated the growth of the use of sign language interpreting in theatres across Britain. The increasing use of British Sign Language interpreting for some news programmes on television has made a significant impact on raising levels of awareness of British Sign Language. Awareness has also been raised by some children's television programmes with items presented in sign language such as *Sesame Street*, *Play Days* and *Hand in Hand*. In addition, television programmes specifically for deaf people such as *Listening Eye* (now *Sign On*) and *See Hear* have also raised the profile of deafness, deaf issues and British Sign Language amongst hearing people, as well as being valuable vehicles for conveying information and cultural communication for deaf people. The increased use of subtitling has contributed to hearing people's awareness of these issues.

Films and literature generally have been less successful to date in presenting positive images of deaf people and in raising awareness of deaf issues. In his discussion of the portrayal of deaf people in the film industry John Schulman writes: 'One must calculate that a collective Hollywood is guilty of the perpetration of a pathological view of deafness as a disease and of deaf individuals as abnormal.'

In literature *The Silent Duchess* portrays the silence of a deaf person as enigmatic, and Susan Gregory in her review of deaf people in literature finds deaf people presented usually as 'lonely and isolated' and British Sign Language and the Deaf community as notable only for their invisibility. Brian Grant also explores images of deafness in literature and draws similar conclusions. Colin Dexter, the creator of the television detective Inspector Morse, is deaf and one of his novels portrays a deaf examination board officer who is endangered by his ability to lipread across a crowded room (*The Silent World of Nicholas Quinn*, 1977). Are we waiting for the first deaf detective to change hearing people's views of deafness, just as feminist, black and gay and lesbian detectives have challenged stereotypes? A Sarah Paretsky of deafness might make some difference to the images of deaf and hard of hearing people in the media.

Generally, images of deaf people are improving and there is a greater awareness amongst hearing people. This is largely as a result of the increasing development of Deaf culture and sign language. Some hearing people have contributed to these developments, for example the Princess of Wales's well-publicised learning of sign language and her attendance at the official launch of the British Sign Language Dictionary in 1992.

Not the only differences

Deaf and hard of hearing people are not different from one another simply because of communication, language and culture; they also have all the differences which exist among hearing people:

- religion
- social class
- geographical area, including rural and urban settings
- sexuality
- age-group
- cultural and linguistic community
- sex
- income
- past educational achievement.

Some deaf or hard of hearing people also have disabilities or learning difficulties.

Deaf or hard of hearing people's experience of deafness is mediated by other aspects of their backgrounds, and these other aspects may, in some contexts, be more significant to the person than their deafness. For example a Deaf Asian Women's Group in South London discussed whether their main source of identity was their deafness, their Asian cultural background or their experiences as women. All three factors were very significant in their lives, both for how they see themselves and how others see them. People's social, cultural and class backgrounds (as well as age, sex, etc.) influence the extent to which they are likely to engage in any form of adult learning or are likely to be non-participants.

The factors which affect participation and non-participation in adult education, and practical ways of involving traditionally non-participant groups in adult learning are explored fully in *Education's for Other People* (McGivney, 1990). There is some discussion of the ways in which deaf and hard of hearing people's backgrounds can act as barriers to their participation in adult education and ways of involving them as learners in Chapter 4, which considers barriers to access.

Voluntary organisations

There are many different national and local Deaf and hard of hearing associations and voluntary organisations. Deaf or hard of hearing adults will usually associate themselves with the one(s) which most closely relate to their own self-identity as a Deaf or hard of hearing person. The range of organisations is discussed in detail in Chapter 6.

The number of deaf and hard of hearing people

As noted earlier, the Medical Research Council's Institute of Hearing Research estimated in 1988 that there were some seven and a half million people who have difficulty with their hearing, about 17 per cent of the population. However, it is felt that there is a need for more research into the number of deaf people and of people with different kinds of hearing loss. The 1992 Commission of Enquiry on Human Aids to Communication which looked at the communication needs of deaf people could not find a reliable way of counting accurately how many people needed to use communication support. Figures used are usually derived from the Medical Research Council's research and the Office of Population Censuses and Surveys (OPCS) 1988 Disability Survey. Davis (1987) felt that the figures used tend to underestimate the number of people in Britain with a hearing loss, even though hearing loss is the second most common disability. The following list gives some of the most salient figures:

- one in a thousand people are born deaf
- 50,000 people use British Sign Language
- 5 million people over 60 years old have difficulty hearing
- the majority of people over 70 have difficulty hearing.

Adult education providers can find out information about the numbers of deaf people in their area by seeking advice from local deaf organisations, Social Services departments and possibly the Health Authority. There may well be local research to draw on about the deaf community. For example, one Midlands authority recently conducted a survey to find out the number of deaf-blind people and what their needs are. This kind of information can then be used to guide the development of suitable educational provision and establish the numbers of people who may be interested in such provision.

2

Language and Communication

Languages and commmunication used by deaf and hard of hearing people

Preferred language and communication

The communication needs of deaf and hard of hearing people

Definitions of human aids to communication

British Sign Language interpreter training

Training for communicators

Providing the most relevant communication support

Language and communication are the central issues in learning for adults who are deaf or hard of hearing. The deaf or hard of hearing person will be clear about how they want to communicate and will let the hearing person know. This needs to be established first of all. Deaf and hard of hearing people are used to adapting to hearing people's communication, spending most of their time in a hearing world. A hearing person might be meeting a deaf or hard of hearing person for the first time and will need to change their communication in order to meet the other person half-way. The same thing applies to lipspeakers and notetakers and other means of communication support. Both sides need the communication support. What form the communication takes depends on whether the deaf or hard of hearing person uses British Sign Language. There are deaf people who use sign language and a larger number of hard of hearing people who do not. The successful delivery of adult learning to people who are deaf or hard of hearing depends on the availability of a variety of means of communication support.

Deaf and hard of hearing adults do not all use the same language; some deaf adults use British Sign Language but most hard of hearing adults and some deaf adults use English and do not understand British Sign Language. Some deaf and hard of hearing adults use only other spoken languages, such as Urdu or Hindi. A hearing person should not feel afraid to ask which language(s) a deaf or hard of hearing person uses and which they prefer to use, or to ask if interpreting/communication support is needed and if so what kind might be the most appropriate. Respecting and responding to the language and communication preferences of deaf and hard of hearing adult learners is a fundamental requirement for providing learning opportunities.

Languages and communication used by deaf and hard of hearing people

British Sign Language

British Sign Language is mainly used by Deaf people. It is a language in its own right, with its own grammar distinct from English. It is a visual, not a spoken language, and there is no conventional written form, although notations are used in specialist areas of work. It has long historical roots but was suppressed in 1880 after the Milan Convention of hearing teachers of deaf children, which shifted the emphasis to the spoken and written and banned sign language in schools. This meant that during this century education for most deaf children has been oral. However, since the 1970s, partly as a result of the low language and literacy development of deaf people educated orally (Conrad, 1979 found that deaf children left school with an average reading age of eight and three-quarters) and partly because of increased interest in and recognition of the importance of British Sign Language as a language amongst the Deaf and hearing communities, there has been an upsurge in the use and the development of British Sign Language. Although British Sign Language is not yet recognised by government as an official language, as it is in Sweden and indeed by the European Community, the publication of the first British Sign Language/English dictionary in 1992 after 10 years' work at the University of Durham was an important achievement in the wider recognition of British Sign Language. Earlier linguistic research into sign language during the 1970s and 1980s (for example Brennan, Colville and Lawson, 1984 and Woll, Kyle and Deuchar, 1981) has been very important in establishing sign language as a language, and has built on the work of William Stokoe in the USA.

British Sign Language is central to Deaf culture and the Deaf community as the conveyor of Deaf culture and community and as the prime means for communication and development of the culture. Teaching in British Sign Language is increasingly common for children and for adults and several authorities or institutions have bilingual policies, for example Leeds Education Authority and the Royal School for the Deaf in Derby. British Sign Language is seen by those who use it as their first language, with English as a second language.

British Sign Language, like other languages, has its own dialects. Just as with spoken language, an adult from Cornwall using British Sign Language will use the language differently from someone from Newcastle; numbers, for example, may be signed differently. In addition each country has its own sign language, although there is an international sign language and deaf people from different countries can generally communicate far more easily than hearing people. Each country's sign language has its own dialects. In the United States, for example, there are differences between black and white signing (Nuru, 1993). Black signing has its own distinctive characteristics and form, and black Deaf people can often code-switch and sign black or white. There are similar black and white signing 'codes' in the UK. Gay and lesbian deaf communities also have distinctive sign language dialects.

British Sign Language users usually define themselves as Deaf with a capital D, and see themselves as part of the Deaf community and Deaf culture. Deaf people are more likely to be involved in Deaf drama, poetry, politics and sports. Deaf culture is becoming more widely recognised and appreciated by hearing people, partly through famous Deaf artists such as Dorothy Miles, a Deaf poet who also contributed to Deaf drama and the development of British Sign Language. Trevor Landell and Damien Robinson are well-known Deaf painters, and various Deaf artists perform at Deaf festivals and at the National Deaf Children's Society annual arts events.

Finger spelling

Finger spelling is a method of communication which involves making a shape with your hand to represent a letter of the alphabet. It is easy to use and to learn. It can give 'clues' to the beginning of words when other methods of communication are being used, for example people and place names or a new product. Some older Deaf people finger spell whole sentences using English words and grammar. Finger spelling is more widely used in Scotland.

Deaf-blind people's communication

Deaf-blind people may use British Sign Language. The deaf-blind person puts their hand over the interpreter's hands as they sign. Some deaf-blind people use finger spelling modified for use on the palm of the hand, or trace out capital letters on the palm of the hand. Others may prefer to sit very close if they have some vision or hearing and follow either by lipreading or signing. At large Deaf conferences there is often an inter-

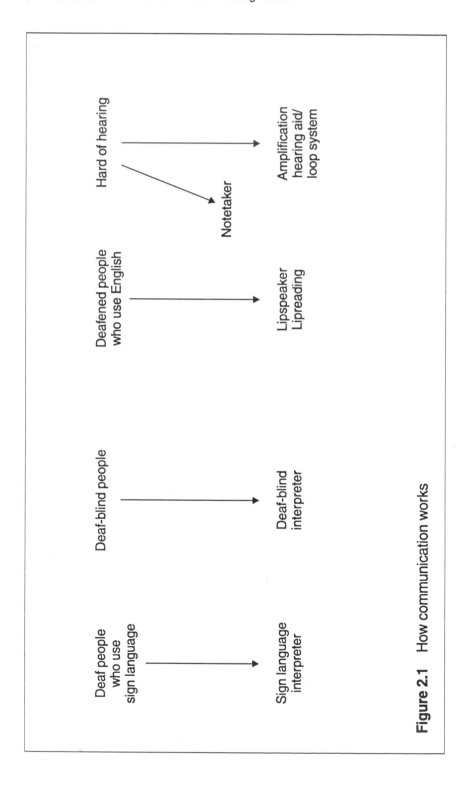

Figure 2.1   How communication works

preter with a small group of deaf-blind delegates following sign language in this way.

Knowing the finger spelling alphabet is useful when meeting a deaf-blind person, as the adaptations to it are small and a conversation can be conducted even if it is very slow at first. If the person has some vision, notetaking can be used with large letters.

Hard of hearing and deafened people's communication

People who have some hearing and/or who become deaf when they are older often have English as their preferred language, using lipreading. Hard of hearing people are sometimes able to maximise their hearing using hearing aids. Some two and a half million people in the United Kingdom have hearing aids (Medical Research Council Institute of Hearing Research). However, not everyone who is hard of hearing can benefit from a hearing aid. For those who can, in many contexts it is difficult to follow speech, for example if there is noise in the background such as music or groups of people chatting, a crisp packet or newspaper being rustled. A hearing aid amplifies everything, not just the voice you want to hear.

Deafened people also usually prefer English, seeing themselves as part of the hearing world, with English as their first language. They may opt for lipreading or writing things down. Lipreading is not easy to learn and it relies on some guesswork related to context. Some people speak with their hand over their mouth and turn their head away so it is not possible to see their lips all the time. Clear speech, facing the person lipreading, is needed to make lipreading possible. Very few people who become deaf later in life choose to learn sign language, although in America, Scandinavia and Germany it is more common for people who become deaf to use sign-supported spoken language. Sign-supported English is different from British Sign Language. It is governed by the grammar and logic of English rather than sign language, and the signing gives visual clues to help the person understand spoken English.

Preferred language and communication

It is important to remember that there are variations in the methods of communication preferred by individuals who are deaf or hard of hearing; not all deaf people use British Sign Language. Some deaf people have grown up in hearing homes and/or schools and have had an oral education in which they have been taught to use lipreading and speech. For these deaf people English may be their preferred language, although some may use British Sign Language, which they have specially learnt later in life to communicate with other deaf people. People who prefer to use English are usually referred to as oral deaf people.

It is important that educational providers do not assume that because someone is deaf or hard of hearing they will use the method of communication most common to that group. Provision and support for deaf and hard of hearing adults needs to be informed by individuals' preferred language or communication.

The communication needs of deaf and hard of hearing people

A Commission of Enquiry into Human Aids to Communication was set up in 1990 to study the communication needs of deaf and hard of hearing people. A panel of the four major organisations for deaf people – the British Association for the Hard of Hearing (BAHOH, now Hearing Concern), the British Deaf Association (BDA), the National Deaf Children's Association (NDCS) and the Royal National Institute for Deaf People (RNID) – produced in 1992 a report, *Communication Is Your Responsibility,* which is the definitive document and should guide and inform all those working with deaf and hard of hearing people. The Panel of Four has now been replaced by the United Kingdom Council on Deafness.

The Commission focused on human aids to communication, that is those people who provide language and communication between hearing people and deaf and hard of hearing people. The issues considered fall into two categories:

- access to spoken language using sign language
- access to spoken language using different strategies based on either visual clues, or text systems or other technology.

The Commission uses the term Human Aids to Communication (HACs) to cover:

- sign language interpreters
- communicators
- interpreters for deaf-blind people
- cued speech facilitators
- notetakers/machine shorthand writers/computer aided transcription operators/subtitlers.

The Commission distinguishes between recognised Human Aids to Communication and those who might be learning language and communication skills but are not at the required stage for recognition. The Commission argues for official recognition arrangements and a standardisation and professionalisation of Human Aids to Communication, with clear national regulatory and registration networks.

Definitions of Human Aids to Communication

(Taken from the Commission of Enquiry into Human Aids to Communication, March 1992.)

Definitions are arranged in two groups:

- definitions of people who are to be regarded as HACs;

- definitions of people who are not to be regarded as HACs.

Definitions of people who are HACs:

A SIGN LANGUAGE INTERPRETER is a person

- who is fluent in sign language and English;

- who is able to function in all situations and varieties of both languages;

- who is trained in the specific interpreting skills of receiving and understanding information in the source language (whether sign language or English), and transmitting this in the target language (whether sign language or English);

- who is trained in interpreting strategies and professional ethics;

- who is a Member of the Register of Sign Language Interpreters following a formal Interpreter's Examination; and

- is eligible to receive payment as a registered sign language interpreter from public funds.

A TRAINEE SIGN LANGUAGE INTERPRETER is a person

- who is fluent in sign language and English (minimum stage III in Sign Language Communication Skills);

- who is registered as a Trainee Sign Language Interpreter with CACDP or SASLI, and/or on a recognised interpreter training course;

- who is eligible for payment as a Registered Trainee Sign Language Interpreter from public funds.

NB: Both CACDP/SASLI will need to create a register to cover the registration of interpreters and trainee interpreters for deaf-blind people. Meanwhile we suggest a definition for an interpreter for deaf-blind people.

A DEAF-BLIND INTERPRETER is a person

- who is fluent in English and all varieties of deaf-blind communication;
- who is able to interpret accurately at whatever speed required by the deaf-blind person;
- who is able to function in all situations in English and deaf-blind communication;
- who is trained in the specific interpreting skills of receiving and understanding information in the source language (whether deaf-blind communication or English), and transmitting this in the target language (whether deaf-blind communication or English);
- who is trained in interpreting strategies and professional ethics;
- who is a Member of the Register of Deaf-Blind Interpreters following a formal Interpreter's Examination;
- who is eligible to receive payment as a registered Deaf-Blind Interpreter from public funds.

At the appropriate time a definition needs to be established for a trainee interpreter for deaf-blind people.

A LEVEL 3 LIPSPEAKER

- is expected to work in any setting, such as medical, legal or education;
- is registered as a Level 3 Lipspeaker on the Register of Lipspeakers;
- is eligible for payment as a HAC in all settings from public funds.

A LEVEL 2 LIPSPEAKER

- has advanced listening and lipspeaking skills;
- works with individual users in a wider range of settings;
- works with both individual users as well as groups of users in a variety of settings;
- is registered as a Level 2 Lipspeaker on the Register of Lipspeakers;
- is eligible for payment as a HAC in professional and informal settings from public funds.

A LEVEL 1 LIPSPEAKER

- has listening and lipspeaking skills;

- works with individual users on a one to one basis in a limited range of settings, for example telephone work or informal meetings of deaf people;

- is registered as a Level 1 Lipspeaker on the Register of Lipspeakers;

- is eligible for payment as a HAC in informal settings from public funds.

A COMPUTER AIDED TRANSCRIPTION OPERATOR is a person

- who provides a computerised form of notetaking which allows a verbatim record of what is said to be shown instantly on a monitor or on a large screen;

- who is a member of the Institute of Shorthand Writers;

- who has received training in 'live mode' work and so is eligible to be paid as a HAC from public funds.

A CUED SPEECH FACILITATOR is a person

- who can cue and say any word in his/her national language;

- who holds a Certificate of Proficiency.

A NOTETAKER is a person

- who takes notes for users by summarising what has been said either verbatim or in note form.

NB: The roles of cued speech facilitators and of notetakers will need to be evaluated before final decisions are made on registration, training, fees or salaries.

A SUBTITLER is a person

- who is used in a variety of situations to produce text for foreign films and television programmes as well as for users through teletext subtitles;

- who is trained and employed in the private sector.

Definitions of people who are not HACs:

A STAGE I HOLDER IN SIGN COMMUNICATION SKILLS is regarded as a person

- who can conduct a basic, short conversation with a deaf person using sign language;

- whose use of sign language grammar and vocabulary range is limited;

- whose contact and experience of deaf people is limited;

- who is not eligible to act even as an unqualified HAC after 1 January 1992.

A STAGE II HOLDER IN SIGN COMMUNICATION SKILLS is regarded as a person

- whose receptive and expressive skill may enable them to deal with most everyday conversational settings;

- who should be starting to produce simple sign language constructions effectively;

- who has a wider knowledge and experience of the Deaf community;

- who is not eligible to act even as an unqualified HAC after 1 January 1994.

A STAGE III HOLDER IN SIGN COMMUNICATION SKILLS is a person

- who has obtained a near fluency in the use of sign language both expressively and receptively;

- who has a knowledge of variations in the structure of British Sign Language and command of regional sign language variations;

- who has extensive knowledge and experience of mixing with the Deaf community;

- who is eligible to be registered as a Trainee Sign Language Interpreter;

- who is not eligible to act even as an unqualified HAC after 1 January 1995.

A DEAF-BLIND FACILITATOR is a person

- who can communicate with a range of deaf-blind people;

- who has the CACDP Certificate in Deaf-Blind Communications;

- who is only eligible to act as a HAC if qualified to do so as a HAC and if his/her name appears on the relevant register.

A GUIDE HELPER is a person

- who can communicate with deaf-blind people;

- whose primary function is to build up a relationship with a deaf-blind person on a one to one basis;

- who has the CACDP Certificate in Deaf-Blind Communication;

- who is only eligible to act as a HAC if qualified to do so as a HAC and if his/her name appears on the relevant register.

A COMMUNICATION SUPPORT WORKER IN FURTHER EDUCA-TION is a person

- who is employed as a member of a multidisciplinary team in a dedicated Post 16 Service for hearing impaired students (users);

- who is trained in a variety of communication, linguistic and tutoring skills;

- who supports students in situations where a HAC is not appropriate;

- who is only eligible to act as a HAC if qualified to do so as a HAC and if his/her name appears on the relevant register.

This concludes the list of definitions from the HAC report.

Recommendations

The Commission made a number of recommendations which affect adult education.

1. The Department of Education and Science extend the disabled students' allowance to cover HAC users on all full-time and part-time courses. (1992 rates – up to £1,100 for any course, up to £4,430 p.a. for non-medical helpers, up to £3,325 per course for major items of specialist equipment.)

2. The term Communicator be dropped (see Further Education below).

3. The term Stage III Communicator be replaced by Trainee Sign Language Interpreters for those:

   - registered as a trainee with CACDP/SASLI; and/or

   - on a recognised interpreter training course (CACDP will need to create a trainee category on their register).

4. The term Sign Language Interpreter only be used by Registered Sign Language Interpreters.

Further Education

5. The definition Communication Support Worker be adopted as a replacement for Communicators in Further Education in situations where a HAC is inappropriate.
   They are only eligible to act as HACs if qualified to do so as a HAC and if their name appears on the relevant register.

6. Notetakers be recognised as HACs and be paid as HACs from public funds (for example under the provisions of the Disabled Students' Allowance), then notetakers should be trained and qualified as HACs.

7. Appropriately trained CAT operators be regarded as HACs in professional settings and so eligible for payment from public funds.

8. Registered Level 2 and Level 3 Lipspeakers be regarded as HACs in professional settings and so eligible for payment as a HAC from public funds.

9. Deaf-blindness/dual sensory disability be recognised as a separate disability and not tucked away behind deafness and blindness. Authorities recognise that all staff and carers need training in deaf-blind communication skills. Authorities recognise that the

communication needs of deaf-blind people are unique to each individual.

10. Lipreading teachers should be seen as professionals with communication skills, but not HACs.

Accompanying these recommendations is a phased change-over period for five years whilst 'unqualified people become qualified'. Thirty regional communication support units are recommended to be set up. (The training scheme is recommended to be linked to the NVQ training.) It does mean that those people working in adult education providing communication support may be in a difficult position during this transition phase.

The wider implications for adult education are to be found in the recommendations that, as a general principle:

11. All professionals or employers meeting (HAC) users in the course of their employment:

- accept requests from users for a qualified HAC in situations where accurate communication is essential

- have training in deaf awareness and basic communication skills and strategies.

These should mean providing those resources throughout adult education. Clearly the Commission is only able to make recommendations, but the overall aim is that of providing training and registration of HACs and the recognition of any adult education which is accessible to all those adults who wish to learn.
It means that:

- a choice of HAC who is properly qualified and registered will have to be provided and paid for

- a proper training for those HACs will need to be provided

- the issue of 'communication support workers' in FE rather side-steps the question of what will happen in areas where there are no qualified and registered HACs available

- further specialist training for HACs in adult education is urgently needed.

The Commission of Enquiry has had little time to make an impact on legislation. If its recommendations are taken up then it will cause great changes, particularly if funding for the use and training of HACs became possible. The professionalisation of British Sign Language interpreting, for example, is particularly significant for adult learning, where most language support is not provided by qualified interpreters but by 'communicators' or support lecturers/tutors. This report has left concern about the existing patchwork of provision and what will happen in any period of transition. It also fails to discuss adult learning in any detail. Before discussing the implications for adult learning, what are the issues for both BSL and English?

British Sign Language interpreter training

Training for interpreters is vital if the quality and availability of suitably skilled interpreters are to be enhanced. Increased training opportunities and clearer recognition frameworks are vital if the recommendations in the Commission of Enquiry's Report on Human Aids to Communication are implemented. Adult education services are often the main providers of British Sign Language teaching at introductory levels and so need to be aware of any changing trends in training for British Sign Language interpreting. Adult education providers need to be aware of changing requirements for using qualified interpreters so that they are able to support deaf or hard of hearing adult students across subject areas with suitably qualified Human Aids to Communication.

Structured training with courses at different levels is relatively new in the UK, and there is a lack of training opportunities at advanced levels. Currently there are advanced interpreter training courses only at Bristol, Durham and Wolverhampton universities. The route to becoming an interpreter is via stages 1, 2 and 3 examinations in British Sign Language run by the Council for the Advancement of Communication with Deaf People (CACDP). CACDP holds a register of qualified interpreters in England, Wales and Northern Ireland, and the Scottish Association of Sign Language Interpreters (SASLI) holds the register for Scotland. To register, a person has to have completed stage 3 examinations and passed the CACDP or SASLI registration examinations. In 1990 there were 102 qualified sign language interpreters in the UK, of whom 23 worked full-time (12 freelance, 11 employed) and 61 part-time freelance (Commission's Report, 1992).

A number of providers run stage 1 and stage 2 sign language courses, including the Royal National Institute for Deaf People, many local education authority adult education providers and local voluntary organisations for the Deaf.

There are also some short specialist 'top-up' or post-qualification courses such as the legal, health and other profession-related courses run by the Royal National Institute for Deaf People, the British Deaf Association and the Royal Association of the Deaf. Bristol University's Department of Continuing Education also runs weekend professional skills courses for interpreters on topics such as assertion training, time and stress management and working in the Deaf community as the child of Deaf parents.

Training for communicators/communication support workers

The Commission of Enquiry into Human Aids to Communication recommended that the term 'Communicator' is replaced by 'Communication Support Worker', and that these workers should only be used where using a qualified Human Aid to Communication is inappropriate. The Commission aims to concentrate on developing recognised specialist communications training courses such as British Sign Language rather than the more general training for communicators consisting of a one-year BTEC Continuing Education Certificate: Communication Support Workers with Deaf People and including sign language, lip-speaking and deaf-blind communication support. There was also a Bilingual Skills course at Coventry Technical College aimed at developing linguistic and transfer skills in British Sign Language and English for professionals working with Deaf people.

Issues relating to the training of interpreters and communication workers

There is a debate about the advantages and disadvantages of concentrating on training and employment of specialist interpreters using one method or language for communication, and the more generalist communication support workers using several methods. The key issues in the debate include:

- National Vocational Qualifications, which are competence-based and relate to broadly-based training such as communicator training, are seen as less specialist, leading to lower quality interpreting in any specific language or communication method
- sceptics suspect that National Vocational Qualifications are being promoted because they can lead to cheaper and shorter training

rather than having the best interests of the Deaf community as the prime concern

- if interpreter training is centralised and regulated as recommended some argue that it will lead to too few interpreters and so block a whole range of arenas for people, including much adult education, if only fully qualified interpreters can be used
- teachers of the deaf, lecturers supporting deaf students and communications support workers should be seen to have a much broader role in supporting teaching and learning rather than being simply communication supporters, but their professional skills should be recognised and accredited
- support tutors' and interpreters' distinct roles should be kept separate and not confused (social workers with the deaf do not act as interpreters as it can conflict with the therapeutic social work role)
- the primary concern is that deaf and hard of hearing students' communication and learning needs should be met and this may mean using an interpreter and/or a communication support worker
- should the emphasis be on encouraging more Deaf people to become British Sign Language tutors?
- will learning British Sign Language for interest (a subject area which has seen unprecedented growth in adult education in recent years) wither and disappear if sign language teaching becomes geared towards professional training for interpreters?
- if there was a large reduction in the number of adults studying British Sign Language for interest this would mean fewer hearing adults able to communicate at all directly with deaf adults in informal and social settings
- what will happen to the many experienced and qualified communicators who may not want to become interpreters?
- which bodies should award qualifications and be responsible for the accreditation of training: the National Council for Vocational Qualifications, the universities, the professional associations?
- who should fund interpreters in adult education and should interpreters be available for all who need them?
- if resources for interpreters are limited, how should decisions about priority students or subject areas be made?
- how are Deaf people to be involved in making decisions on these kinds of issues so that it is not, as one Deaf man said, a matter of 'Oh there's a choice alright – hearing people choose!'

Training for communication methods where English is the preferred language

There is little if any training available for lipspeakers, notetakers or computer aided transcript (CAT) operators. Lipreading teachers have a similar role to sign language teachers in that they teach deaf or hard of hearing adults skills in lipreading so that they can either directly understand spoken English or understand it through a lipspeaker. Hearing therapists also provide lipreading training. Training for lipspeaking is at three levels and is co-ordinated by the Council for the Advancement of Communication with Deaf People (CACDP) and Hearing Concern.

Issues relating to the training of communications workers where English is the preferred language

There is broad agreement about the need for the development and improvement of training for communications workers where English is the preferred language, but there is discussion around a number of issues including:

- should there be a common core curriculum for communications workers to include areas such as ethics, precising/summarising skills, listening skills, negotiating with users and tutors about how best to offer communication support, agreeing contracts for communication support, etc.?
- should the roles of lipreading tutors and hearing therapists be combined within one profession?
- how can the profile be raised of deaf or hard of hearing people using English as their preferred language so that as a group their presence and needs are not 'invisible' and neglected?
- how can new technology best be harnessed to support communication?
- should sign-supported spoken English be promoted more in the UK?
- who should fund communication support and how should decisions about priorities for the use of scarce resources be made?
- how can the users of communication support where English is the preferred language be involved in the development of services?

Providing the most relevant communication support

Providers of adult learning opportunities need to establish with a student before work begins:

- if the student wants to be taught in British Sign Language and if so with a
  - deaf tutor
  - hearing tutor fluent in sign
  - hearing subject tutor and a British Sign Language interpreter
  - notetaker and interpreter
  - discrete group of Deaf students
- whether the student feels comfortable about using English
- whether the student wants literacy support.

A provider needs to establish with a student before work begins if they prefer English as the medium for teaching and if so whether the student wants support from:

- a lipspeaker
- a sign-supported English interpreter
- a CAT operator
- a notetaker, with an overhead projector or sitting next to them
- any other system.

Conclusion

Different languages are used by deaf and hard of hearing people. It is important to recognise these differences. Communication is a two-way process and the hearing person needs the communication support worker as much as the deaf or hard of hearing person does. The recognition of British Sign Language by the European Community (1988) should go a long way to ensuring minority language status for British Sign Language in this country. Equal value needs to be placed on both British Sign Language and the English-based communication used by deaf, hard of hearing and deafened people in the adult learning process. Deaf, deafened, deaf-blind and hard of hearing people must participate fully in the training and assessment of communication support workers and in the form of communication support used in the learning process.

3

Meeting Communication Needs

Technological aids to communication

Types of technology

People providing language and communication support

Concerns and issues

Providing learning opportunities for any group of people who are culturally distinct, or who have different language and communication needs from the majority, requires a number of basic arrangements, facilities and resources before learning can even begin. This chapter gives a practical guide to meeting the needs of different deaf and hard of hearing adults wanting to participate in learning, and describes some of the people with specialist skills which are needed and the technology and practical aids available to support and enable learning.

There is evidence that deaf and hard of hearing adults are keen to learn and that many providers are keen to provide discrete learning opportunities and suitable support for deaf and hard of hearing adults to join mainstream courses of their choice. However, many providers are not aware of the options and the best ways of making communication possible so that deaf and hard of hearing adults can learn most effectively without communication problems being a barrier to their participation. Although making communications work has resource implications (both human and financial), providers are often prepared to commit resources to enable this group of adults to participate in courses just as their hearing counterparts do. Chapter 8 gives some information about sources of funding (both mainstream and 'special' funding).

Many providers have attracted and used successfully funding from various sources to provide equal learning opportunities for deaf and hard of hearing adults.

Technological aids to communication

Technology can make communication easier for some people who are deaf or hard of hearing. However, technology does not provide a solution for everyone who is deaf. For example, those students who have some hearing may benefit from amplification, whereas for those with no hearing this offers no help. Those who read well may benefit from comprehensive notetaking. Technology can be very expensive and high powered or relatively cheap, simple and very cost effective. A loop system can transform hard of hearing students' and tutors' experience of learning for very little outlay.

Technology can be useful:

- to amplify sound for those people with some hearing who wear hearing aids (loop systems, radio hearing aids)
- to facilitate comprehension in 'real time' (computerised notetaking systems with printing facilities)
- to provide notetaking for reference purposes (computerised note-taking systems with printing facilities)
- to give access to information available to hearing people (television subtitling)
- to provide a medium for conveying sign language in teaching and learning (video recording)
- to facilitate communication for deaf-blind people.

Types of technology

Loop system

How does a loop system work? A wire is placed around the room attached to an amplifier which picks up sounds and passes them directly through the inductive coupler in the hearing aid without sounds having to travel through the air. As someone speaks the sound waves are converted into an electric current which goes around the room in an invisible magnetic field. The current in the loop varies according to the level and types of sounds fed into it. The inductive coupler in the hearing aid picks up the signal from the loop and this is then amplified by the hearing aid. The signals are picked up instantly by the hearing aid and fed directly into the ear. Because sound waves do not have to travel directly through the air the sound is less distorted than is normal through a hearing aid.

On all NHS and on some privately-bought aids, there is a 'T' switch (standing for Telecoil), positioned in between the 'O' and the 'M'. This 'T' switch turns off the microphone setting and activates the telecoil within the hearing aid. The hearing aid user is not physically attached to an amplifier, which can be located around a room or in a small circle worn around the neck. Personal loops around the neck can be used at home for listening to the radio, for a personal tutorial, watching television or listening to tapes, for example, but in teaching situations it is more likely that a larger loop system will be used, extended around the room. One advantage of loop systems is that they cut down on background noise, but they do sometimes suffer from other electric currents interfering with the sensitivity of the coil within the hearing aid. This may mean that a fluorescent light or other piece of electrical equipment such as an overhead projector nearby might cause buzzing. It is important to check the equipment prior to the teaching session; if this is not possible, set up and explain the system to group members in a matter-of-fact way.

Some theatres have loop systems fitted, thus making performances accessible to hearing aid users following a drama or literature course. Some lecture theatres have loop systems too. Using rooms with a built-in loop system is ideal, but it is mainly portable loop systems that are used. Often these can be hired.

Different microphones are suitable for different sorts of teaching settings. Tie-clip or desk-top microphones might be used. Some microphones are multidirectional, which means that the microphone does not have to be passed around to people as they want to speak. However, these are not suitable for all teaching settings. They work better in small groups but are effective in large groups when the technology is of a high standard and the rules of communication are observed.

Setting up the loop system. The person with responsibility for setting up a loop system varies according to the context. In some institutions or centres, there will be a technician to set up the system and ensure it is working correctly. In others it will be the responsibility of learning support tutors or those co-ordinating special needs. Sometimes the tutor may have to set up the system. Students may find themselves having to sort it out if no one else is available, but this should be avoided if possible so that students can concentrate on the learning and providers take responsibility for ensuring that staff can communicate with students.

Using the loop system. The main thing for anyone speaking is to remember that only what is said into the microphone will be heard by the hearing aid user. This means that whoever is speaking must use the microphone. So, for communication to be clear in a group discussion, the microphone must be passed around, while in a lecture a lapel microphone should be attached to the speaker. In a situation where it is inappropriate to pass a microphone around, such as with questions from the floor in a large lecture theatre, information should be repeated, or paraphrased, by the speaker. It is important that the tutor explains to the group how they should use the microphone and the loop system before the session starts so that all know how to use it and there is minimum embarrassment. The tutor can demonstrate, and if possible it is best if the hard of hearing student knows beforehand how the system will work and how the tutor will explain it to the group and feels comfortable with the tutor's plans.

There are some constraints on using the loop in a group where people are unfamiliar with a learning situation or with one another. Some people may feel easier using loops in a stable and highly motivated group. There can be a problem of competing anxieties and competing needs, for example where everyone is new to both the group and adult learning. Suddenly being asked to speak into a microphone can be unnerving. The tutor may make sure that the least difficult or threatening kind of discussions are at the beginning of a session, for example introductions or the tutor giving information, until people get used to the loop system and using a microphone.

Some reactions to using the loop system include:

'I thought I was being tape-recorded. I didn't want to speak into the microphone at first – then I understood later on' (a student in a group with a hard of hearing student).

'In the end it was very helpful passing the mike around in a group discussion, because we all stopped interrupting one another and took it in turns to speak' (a fellow student.).

'It's wonderful for me to use the loop, as it cuts down all the background noise and I can really concentrate on what is being said' (a hard of hearing student).

Things to remember when working with a loop system:

- the loop system does not solve all the difficulties of being deaf or hard of hearing. Basic rules of communication need to be observed and speech should be clear
- a good quality loop is essential. Advice should be sought from knowledgeable contacts
- not everyone who is deaf or hard of hearing can benefit from the use of a loop system. It depends on whether they can use a hearing aid as well as on whether their aid has a 'T' setting
- beware of interference from noisy overhead projectors or fluorescent lighting.

Radio microphone systems

These are used a lot in schools and in further education and they are sometimes given out to individual students for use in adult education. The system involves a receiver and a transmitter with a microphone.

The speaker wears an FM radio transmitter and the hard of hearing person wears the receiver with headphones or a direct link to their hearing aid. The system is more useful for 'talk and chalk' situations than for group discussions, when the radio transmitter has to be passed around to each person who speaks. It is a portable system which the student can take along wherever they go and it is easy to set up. Most hearing impaired services have the systems available for loan.

The system should be turned off during break times so that the hard of hearing student does not continue to hear conversations in the teaching room.

Computerised text systems

There are a number of different computerised text systems, including computerised transcription equipment, computers where a person takes notes, subtitling on visual images such as slides, television and video, text telephones, faxes and electronic mail which print communications using telephone lines. The following paragraphs describe some computer aided transcription (CAT) systems.

Palantype system. The most commonly known system used for deaf people is the Palantype system (Possum Palantype Computer Aided Transcription System). One well-known user is Jack Ashley MP, from 1974 until his retirement in 1991 from the House of Commons. The system was developed by Possum Controls and Southampton University, and is based on court reporting stenography. It incorporates an electronic keyboard for operator input phonetic language, which the computer translates into English, checks spelling and displays the output on a large screen or VDU. Palantype takes place in real time so the deaf or hard of hearing person can read words on the monitor almost as they are spoken if the operator who inputs the shorthand works at the same pace as the people speaking, which they usually can.

A two-week training course is run for Palantype operating at Slough (Possum Controls Ltd), with course assessment and examination by correspondence. The qualification is issued by the Institute of Shorthand Writers.

Computerised text systems are used in the courts and in the Houses of Parliament, but rarely in education. Currently Palantype equipment is expensive (around £6,000 at 1993 prices), and a qualified operator costs £75 per day at 1993 prices. It is probably only an option at the moment for people and organisations with a good level of resources. Realistically, Palantype is only available to very few people, and in most services cannot be provided for adult learners.

Hilinc system. This is a newly developing computer aided transcription service. It is a visual text display system based on a video unit which accepts computer generated text (either by an operator or directly from a prepared file), and displays it on a large screen for the viewer to read. This display can be in the form of text-only display or text video.

Hilinc is cheaper than the Palantype machine for the basic technical unit and uses a standard IBM PC or compatible computer. There are no set operator fees yet. Likewise, there is no set training. An experienced typist listens and types in what she or he hears, or alternatively uses a prepared text.

This system is relatively new and untried, but it is an attempt to introduce a system cheaper than Palantype. However, it does depend on having an experienced typist who is familiar with the topic and language and knows how to precis information and is aware of the ethics of interpreting.

Electronic notepads and lap-top personal computers. These are a new development in computerised text systems which are, at present, used by some police services to take statements, by surgeons in operating theatres to take notes and increasingly by people to take notes in meetings or lectures, etc. For a deaf or hard of hearing person a hearing typist needs to type at the same speed as the speech or to summarise information and type it, so that the deaf or hard of hearing person can read at the same time on the display screen. Advantages are that notebooks and lap-tops are relatively inexpensive and becoming cheaper, and are fairly familiar equipment to tutors and other students. Prepared information on floppy disk can be input if software is compatible, and with access to a printer the student could also use the notepad or lap-top for written work. Notetaking using a notebook or lap-top computer can be in real time (as people speak), and the text can be saved and then retrieved at a later time for reference. This does depend on having a hearing typist who can take notes and, as with a Hilinc system, is familiar with the language and can summarise information effectively. As keyboard/typing skills become more common it may be possible to find volunteers or fellow students to use this system. This portable system might well be developed to be used for students in adult education.

Subtitling of television and videos

Television and videos can improve access to information of all kinds, from health issues, current affairs and nature, to DIY and social issues in general television broadcasting, to specific educational broadcasting such as the Learning Channel and the Open University.

Two methods are used for subtitling in broadcasting:

- real time subtitling based on stenography
- the less expensive ENCAPS method which uses manually-cued speech subtitling which the operator keys out during the programme.

In the United States, real time stenography subtitling is a daily occurrence. By 1998 there was a commitment in the United Kingdom to subtitle 50 per cent of all television programmes, mainly as the result of the Deaf Broadcasting Council's 10-year battle to achieve what they consider to be a basic right to information.

Ceefax and Teletext on television provide printed information on a wide range of topics. Ceefax runs an information magazine for deaf and hard of hearing people, *Read Hear*, which runs daily and is changed twice weekly. Channel 4 has *Deafview*. Ceefax and teletext are very accessible to those deaf and hard of hearing people who have televisions with these functions. Videos with subtitles are becoming more common and also offer access to a range of information and education.

Text telephones, videophones, faxes and electronic mail

Text and videophones, faxes and electronic mail are all interactive communication systems with telephone lines. They are all potentially accessible as most homes and organisations have a telephone line. Hearing students take for granted being able to telephone for information about a course in which they are interested and being informed by telephone if a class is cancelled. A text telephone can provide the means for deaf and hard of hearing people to have access to communication and information in a way that is confidential, direct and available. The person types their message and this is then printed out on the receiving telephone. The first public text telephone call box was opened at King's Cross station, London in 1993.

Training courses on how to use text telephones are run by Teletec International, which markets Minicom text telephones, and Portaview, another text telephone supplier. Adult education needs to become part of the growing network of text telephones.

Typetalk. Typetalk is a Liverpool-based special relay telephone service, similar to text telephones, which means that deaf, hard of hearing and deaf-blind subscribers can type in on a text telephone, the hearing operator speaks to the hearing person on the other end and then types back the reply. It is jointly funded by British Telecom, Liverpool City Council and the Royal National Institute for Deaf People. It opens up the telephone network for deaf and hard of hearing people but has the limitation of lack of confidentiality as everything goes through the operator; in addition, it is text-based and literacy is sometimes a problem for British Sign Language users.

Video telephones and electronic mail. Video telephones are something which Deaf people who use British Sign Language and deaf and hard of hearing people who lipread are hoping will be developed to the point where sign language conversations are possible by telephone, with lipreading also a possibility. At present videophones are small and show only the face, making sign language difficult. They are also quite expensive (some £800 for two videophones) but it is expected that they will come down in price. Some development work is being done on the use of videophones for deaf and hard of hearing adults (for example the Royal National Institute for Deaf People and Cheshire Deaf Society's RACE initiative). Faxes similarly are now coming down in price and are more frequently used, and accessible electronic mail using personal computers and a modem link with the telephone system is being developed and used more widely. Electronic mail can help deaf and hard of hearing adults communicate in writing using the phone lines.

Amplification for telephones

Amplified handsets are useful for people using hearing aids and are relatively inexpensive to install. The 'T' switch on a hearing aid makes it possible for a hard of hearing person to use the telephone and adjust the volume. A portable telephone amplifier can also be made available to students.

Other technology and aids

Other aids which are useful in adult learning for people who are deaf or hard of hearing include such 'low tech' and low cost items as:

- carbon note copying
- flip charts
- flashlight for interpreting or lipreading in the dark, for example when slides are shown
- overhead projector with a continuous film for notetaking
- tape recorder with a tone adjuster, repayable at different speeds
- microwriters.

Aids for non-teaching purposes are a basic requirement for safety in an institution, including flashing fire alarms and flashing light or vibrating alarms in residential rooms. There are also tactile acoustic monitors for fire alarms to be worn on the wrist.

Technological aids for deaf-blind communication

For deaf-blind people there are a number of technological devices. To aid communication there is the Hand Tapper – an electronic 'glove' which facilitates communication. It is being developed at University College London with the support of SENSE (Deaf, Blind and Rubella Association). There is also the Hasicom, a text telephone for deaf-blind people. Large print numbers are also available on telephones for those with visual problems.

Technological development and support

Considerable development in technological aids has taken place, particularly at Southampton, Reading, Leeds and Bristol universities and University College London. There is a European Deaf-fax Unit, a Deaf Research and Development Centre on Deafness/Disability and a computer electronic mail system at Reading University. Leeds University has developed subtitling systems for television and notetaking. Moray House at Heriot Watt University has developed a range of new technology for deaf people in education.

The Cheshire Deaf Society runs a Bulletin Board which provides an information service. The Royal National Institute for Deaf People has a Technical Awareness Service at its London office and the National Deaf Children's Society has a Centre for Information and Technology in Birmingham, which is a useful contact point for technology.

People providing language and communication support

Language and communication support for deaf and hard of hearing people focuses on British Sign Language and spoken and written language.

English and other written or spoken languages

Most teaching in adult educational opportunities uses English, but there is also a substantial and growing area of teaching in community languages, for example sewing in Gujarati, DIY in Bengali. Deaf and hard of hearing adults operating in a language other than English need the same technological and Human Aids to Communication but these must be appropriate for that language, for example using a notetaker who can write in Bengali, using a lap-top computer with Punjabi language software. Some deaf adults may also use sign languages other than British Sign Language.

Lipspeakers

Lipspeaking began in 1949 at the British Association for the Hard of Hearing (BAHOH; now Hearing Concern) in Darlington as a support for social events. Lipspeakers (called oral interpreters in the USA) provide a clear, slower spoken version of what is being said by the main speaker. They are usually used by people who are profoundly deaf or deafened as adults and so use English. Lipspeaking has moved from a voluntary to a professional role. Training is run by Hearing Concern, the Council for the Advancement of Communication with Deaf People (CACDP) and the Department for Education. Registers of lipspeakers with qualifications are held by these bodies. Most lipspeakers have to pay for their own training, which limits the number of people prepared to train, and there is a blockage at level two training, where 20 hours' practice is needed. Some developments are needed, and a common curriculum for training is being established. There is a code of practice and ethics as for interpreters. As a method of communication lipspeaking is not as well established as sign language, and availability is limited. The health promotion initiative 'Aids Ahead' which provides information for deaf people has extended its services to include lipspeakers and this may help stimulate wider use of lipspeaking. Use of lipspeakers is rare in educational settings but could be extended. Lipspeakers should be paid. It can be problematic to identify both funding and suitably qualified and experienced lipspeakers. Ideally a lipspeaker would have some knowledge of the subject area taught. It is always useful to provide lecture notes, handouts, etc. to the lipspeaker (as well as the students) before a teaching session so that they are familiar with the subject area and the structure of the session. Lipreading is tiring and ideally there should be a short rest every half hour or so.

Notetakers

A personal notetaker sits next to the deaf or hard of hearing person and notes what is said, especially key points. Another way is for the notetaker to sit and write on an overhead projector at the front of the group. Deaf and hard of hearing adults often find using a notetaker more restful than lipreading.

There is a shortage of notetakers and very little systematic training or funding for training or employing them. The University of Durham's Hearing Impaired Student Support Service uses professional notetakers, but this is unusual. Mostly notetakers are volunteers, possibly a fellow student in the class. However, training in the skills of precising information, using clear English and the basic ethics of interpreting is important. In a class with a British Sign Language interpreter a Deaf person would also need a notetaker as it is impossible to watch an interpreter and take notes at the same time.

Interpreters

Deaf people who use British Sign Language will need a sign language interpreter if teaching is in English or another language. Occasionally an interpreter may be used where the teaching is in British Sign Language so that a hard of hearing adult using English can participate. Interpreters act as a channel between the two languages, for both deaf and hearing people.

An interpreter:

- stands between the two parties, representing neither
- should be functionally bilingual
- is concerned with meaning and how this is to be represented in each language
- works in real time, interpreting at the same time as speech
- works from a 'source' language into a 'target' language, conveying the appropriate meaning and intent
- is very visible, unlike spoken language interpreters, which adds additional pressure to the role (Kyle, 1991).

There is recognised training for sign language interpreting, the Council for the Advancement of Communication with Deaf People (CACDP) stages one, two and three. (See Chapter 2 for a full account of this.)

Students on the level three course are trainee interpreters and those who have completed stage three can register as qualified interpreters. Communicators are interpreters who are not fully qualified, and it has been recommended by the Commission of Enquiry into Human Aids and Communication that only fully qualified British Sign Language interpreters (that is those who have completed stage three training and registered) should be recognised as interpreters because of the high level skills required and the complexity of the task. The Commission also recommended that there should be registered trainee interpreters/communication support workers who are on the stage three course. There are debates about which terms to use (trainee interpreters or communicators), which causes some confusion. In 1990 there were only 102 qualified sign language interpreters and it was estimated in 1991 that there were over 100 communicators working in the post-16 sector, mostly in further education colleges (Green and Nickerson, 1992). There is an estimated British Sign Language population of some 50,000.

Support tutors/lecturers for deaf students

As well as communication support the role of learning support is important for working with deaf and hard of hearing adults. Over 90 Local Education Authorities have specialist support posts for work with deaf people in the post-16 sector. Many of the tutors come from a background of teaching deaf children and may now belong to the National Association for Tertiary Education and Deaf People (NATED) or the British Association of Teachers of the Deaf (BATOD).

Other staff

Social workers with deaf people can be useful contacts for recruitment, as well as sometimes being involved in providing support for deaf adults who want to study, for example helping with advice on fees, travel, interpreters, childcare, etc.

Hearing therapists. Hearing therapy is a relatively new profession and therapists usually work in hospitals, providing support for those with acquired deafness. Again they may help with recruitment of students and help contribute to teaching, especially lipreading classes, hearing tactics and giving information and practice for deaf and hard of hearing adults on using technology and different kinds of aids to communication.

Graphic visualisers. Some Local Education Authorities have graphic visualiser posts, for example Humberside Hearing Support Service, who produce teaching materials with plenty of visual information.

Video technicians. These can be very helpful when showing deaf and hard of hearing students how to make videos as a way of presenting information in British Sign Language and for assessment of students using British Sign Language.

Concerns and issues about technological and human aids communication

The main issues include:

- volunteers or paid workers?
- people with good basic or intermediate skills in interpreting or highly trained paid professionals?
- costs of different technological or human aids to communication
- identifying the best methods of communication support which are affordable
- the role of specialist units or staff and drawing on expertise or practical support from other agencies.

In an ideal world a provider would have a variety of services and resources on offer for deaf and hard of hearing adults, but in reality providers have to operate within very limited budgets.

Volunteers can make a valuable contribution, for example as notetakers, but it is expensive to 'skill' volunteers by providing training and support, and without training the quality of volunteers' work is uncertain. Volunteers are not a 'no cost' option. However, if a deaf or hard of hearing person has access to some interpreter time they may be more likely to prioritise it for visits to the doctor or the housing office for essential survival issues, rather than for educational opportunities. Therefore the use of volunteers may be the only practical way of enabling deaf and hard of hearing adults to participate in education unless the provider has funding for professional staff support, or funding for the student is earmarked to support learning (for example for full-time higher education students).

The Commission of Enquiry into Human Aids to Commication put the case for public investment in support of deaf and hard of hearing adults for different aspects of their lives, including education. Until there is such public investment, although the idea is for the student to have communication support from professionals, there are concerns about applying this too rigidly:

- the cost may be prohibitive, so preventing the student from doing the course at all
- the shortage of qualified interpreters can mean that even if funds are available suitable staff are not, which would also prevent the person taking the course
- the number of staff hours available is likely to be limited by funding and the limited availability of professional interpreters, making it possible for the student to study only one course or to study part-time rather than full-time.

A combination of professional interpreters and trainee volunteers is most likely to be achievable and affordable, permitting specialist support and some direct interpreting where most needed.

Another option is befriending. A befriender is offered a free place on the course to accompany a deaf or hard of hearing person. The befriender provides notetaking or other communication or language support for the deaf or hard of hearing student to help the tutor and other students communicate with the student, and also for the deaf or hard of hearing student to communicate with the tutor and with fellow students. The Norfolk Social Communicator Scheme uses this approach. Issues such as support or training for the befriender need to be addressed. Other issues include the best ways for the tutor and befriender to work together to support the student's learning, decisions on the extent to which the befriender participates in the course as an individual, how the rest of the group use the befriender, making sure the befriender knows the course outline and objectives or concerns, making sure the befriender is aware of any difficult language which might arise, etc.

Training volunteers

The following is a list of the key issues surrounding the training of voluntary human aids to communication. Such training should:

- be run by professional interpreters and/or very experienced communicators
- have a clear core curriculum which would include topics such as
  - listening skills
  - skills of conveying information and meaning accurately
  - skills of precising information

- skills of using ordinary English language and introducing technical terms relevant to the subject
- negotiating and agreeing methods of assisting communication with the deaf or hard of hearing student and with the tutor, including finding out the learning objectives of the course, etc.
- the ethics of interpreting/communicating
- drawing up a contract/agreement about the service offered which spells out their role

- address aspects of access to the course where the volunteer may be needed, for example in the canteen, at reception, registering for exams.

British Sign Language interpreting cannot be done without proper training, as it can lead to the deaf student having inaccurate and incomplete communication. A trainee or fully qualified interpreter should be used.

It is of course essential that providers find out from deaf or hard of hearing students which kinds of aids and communication they would find most suitable and whether they would like to have any opportunity for familiarisation, for example practising using a portable loop system, trying for one or two sessions using a notetaker to see how it works. Providers can draw on specialist advice from hearing support units, national deaf and hard of hearing organisations, etc. or specialist staff such as hearing therapists, qualified British Sign Language interpreters and experienced tutors so that the best possible approaches for meeting the communication needs of deaf and hard of hearing adults are used.

4

Overcoming Barriers to Access

Before and at entry
During a programme of study
At the point of exit
Collaborating to overcome barriers

The previous chapters have focused on issues relating to language and communication and ways of establishing effective methods of communication with deaf and hard of hearing adults so that they can participate fully in adult learning opportunities. Language and communication are fundamental considerations for any provider of adult education wanting to offer opportunities for deaf and hard of hearing adults. However, there are many other barriers to access for deaf and hard of hearing adults. Barriers can occur throughout the learning process:

- before and at the point of entry to a programme of study
- during a programme of study
- at the point of exit from study.

Before and at entry to a programme of study

There are two main kinds of barrier to access for deaf and hard of hearing adults before and at the point of entry. These are:

- practical barriers such as lack of transport, high fees, etc.
- background, past experiences and how people see themselves.

For providers to overcome practical and other barriers it is important that they are well informed and have an understanding of deaf and hard of hearing issues.

The practical barriers are generally fairly straightforward for a provider to address in order to make it possible for deaf and hard of hearing adults to participate in adult learning programmes.

Unsuitable provision

If the kinds of courses and the communication and learning support offered are not suitable or of interest to deaf and hard of hearing adults then even if all other barriers were removed they are unlikely to participate in programmes. The evidence from the NIACE survey (see Appendix 1) suggests that deaf and hard of hearing adults are interested in a wide range of learning opportunities across curriculum areas. (Examples of successful programmes for deaf and hard of hearing adults are given in the next chapter.) It is also clear that there is a demand for some discrete courses for deaf and hard of hearing adults, as well as opportunities for joining integrated classes with suitable language and communication support, for example a notetaker or interpreter. For discrete courses it is essential that careful work is carried out to identify the needs and interests of local deaf and hard of hearing people. This can be done through contacts and discussions with:

- deaf and hard of hearing adults who are potential students, including groups such as Deaf clubs, etc.
- specialist agencies working with deaf and hard of hearing adults such as local centres for deaf people, specialist national organisations such as Skill, the Royal National Institute for Deaf People or the British Deaf Association
- specialist workers with deaf and hard of hearing people such as hearing therapists in the health service, social workers for the deaf
- general providers or agencies who may work with some deaf and hard of hearing adults and be aware of interests and needs, for example adult guidance workers, employers, adult basic education services, etc.

As far as possible deaf and hard of hearing adults who are intended to benefit from the discrete provision should be involved in the planning and setting up of the programme, including decisions about priorities for subjects and about languages used in teaching, for example British Sign Language.

For both discrete provision and for general adult learning opportunities which deaf and hard of hearing adults may want to join it is essential that providers find out the kinds of language, literacy and communication support that may be needed. For example a discrete GCSE English course may be taught in English but the deaf students may need a British Sign Language interpreter. For general programmes it is important that the institution can offer as wide a range as possible of support arrangements so that they can be used according to individual need, for example a portable loop system, a network of trained volunteer notetakers, etc.

Lack of information

Even when a provider offers programmes which are attractive to deaf or hard of hearing adults and there are suitable language, literacy and communication arrangements in place, information about these opportunities may not give all the relevant information, may not be conveyed in appropriate ways or may not reach the right people. Occasionally information may be failing on all three counts. Details of the course content and the methods of teaching should be given, highlighting the aspects which are going to be of particular interest to deaf or hard of hearing adults, such as language and communication support available, parts of the course covering deaf issues, etc. It is also useful to make a general statement about the institution's commitment to providing learning opportunities for deaf and hard of hearing adults and perhaps to give illustrative case studies of past deaf or hard of hearing students to show that 'education is for people like me'. Details of the centre's general facilities for deaf and hard of hearing people should be given, such as amplified telephones, lecture rooms with loop systems, extra tutorials for deaf or hard of hearing students, radio microphones for loan, etc.

Research shows that word of mouth publicity is often the most effective, supported by printed material. All information and publicity needs to be given in an accessible form for deaf and hard of hearing adults. Printed material should use plain English, or other community languages as appropriate, as literacy skills may be a problem for deaf people using British Sign Language. Extensive use of graphics can help convey information. Video prospectuses in sign language are effective and are used as standard publicity by Doncaster College for the Deaf and Derby College for the Deaf. Publicity can be put on television, for example through features or information items on specialist programmes for deaf and hard of hearing people such as *See Hear* on BBC, *Sign On* on Channel 4, and information on Teletext systems on the specialist pages for deaf and hard of hearing adults such as *Read Hear* on BBC and *No Need to Shout* on ITV. The discrete NNEB course for deaf people at Basford Hall, Nottingham was advertised successfully on television.

Any information about courses should include details of key contacts, when they are available and how contact can be made. These people should be well informed about the courses and any facilities or arrangements for deaf and hard of hearing people and they also need to be able to communicate effectively with enquirers, for example using electronic mail, text telephone or British Sign Language in face to face meetings. Several strategies can be used to make sure information about programmes reaches the right people. These can include:

- circulating printed publicity to key contacts in specialist agencies and specialist workers with deaf and hard of hearing adults, as well as to relevant general agencies, ideally with a covering letter which explains the provider's keenness to offer a good range of learning opportunities for deaf and hard of hearing adults and commitment to providing suitable support, etc.
- visits and presentations to local Deaf clubs and centres and other deaf and hard of hearing organisations
- discussing courses and opportunities with key workers who may refer deaf or hard of hearing adults as a follow up to, or coupled with, the printed publicity or British Sign Language video material
- using services aimed at the deaf and hard of hearing communities, for example Teletext, Deaf newsletter and publications such as Hearing Concern's journal, the National Association of Deaf People's journal, the deaf television news run in conjunction with the British Deaf Association on Channel 4
- giving information (signed, spoken or printed) to any existing deaf or hard of hearing students or employees in the service, building on the existing relationships with deaf and hard of hearing people
- working with deaf or hard of hearing students or ex-students or professionals who can act as link people

Lack of guidance

Many deaf or hard of hearing adults may not be sure which kind of learning opportunity is most suitable for them. They may need an opportunity to discuss options with someone who can give impartial information, counselling and advice in relation to opportunities available from different providers. Any guidance services or staff should be able to offer guidance to deaf or hard of hearing adults and have a good information base covering discrete courses, the range of support services different providers have for deaf and hard of hearing people, and any special sources of funding or equipment loans, etc. for deaf and hard of hearing adults. Guidance staff also need to be able to communicate effectively with deaf and hard of hearing adults, either directly or through an interpreter. They need to have a general understanding of deaf and hard of hearing adults' experience and the factors which may influence their participation in learning programmes. Traditionally, educational opportunities for deaf and hard of hearing adults may not have been designed to lead to more advanced education, training or jobs and many deaf and hard of hearing adults may have fairly low expectations and ambitions. Guidance workers play an important role in enabling deaf and hard of hearing people to increase their confidence in their ability to learn and succeed, and to consider higher levels of study which can help them realise their full potential.

Guidance at Newham Community College

The college aims to provide guidance interviews for any new deaf and hard of hearing students through the College's Learning Support Co-ordinator, the Hearing Impaired Support Tutor and the full-time communicator. The College offers:

- a pre-interview meeting with communication support of the deaf or hard of hearing adult's choice
- an interview with communication support
- a guidance meeting with communication support to identify a plan for the future, including which course(s) to do and where this might lead in the longer term
- guidance meetings as needed throughout the programme of study.

Sometimes it is necessary to bring in people with specialist information or skills to contribute to the guidance meetings, for example a course tutor.

Unwelcoming institutions

Many educational institutions are off-putting for adults, especially those who feel they have not been successful in educational institutions in the past, which is true for many deaf and hard of hearing adults. The accessibility of an institution and the welcome it extends to deaf and hard of hearing adults depend to a large extent on the form of communication employed. An institution can have a range of ways for communicating effectively with deaf and hard of hearing adults which demonstrate that they are welcome and that the institution intends to provide good services for them. Forms of communication include:

- text and amplified telephones or use of a Typetalk telephone relay system for the institution's telephone system or public payphone in the institution
- amplified telephones and text telephones, as at the Gallaudet University for Deaf People in Washington. These become available for payphones following British Telecom's trial in five centres during 1993
- reception and telephone staff trained in using text and amplified telephones; for example text telephone has a range of standard abbreviations such as GA for Go Ahead, SK, meaning Stop Keying [end of conversation], or TMW for tomorrow
- reception, catering and ancillary staff and teaching staff who are able to relate to deaf and hard of hearing adults and have undergone training in Deaf awareness and language and communication skills to avoid off-putting experiences for deaf and hard of hearing adults: *'I went in to ask about a class and the receptionist just mumbled. She turned round to answer the telephone and talked to me at the same time. It was hopeless'* (potential deaf learner)
- open days and/or a drop-in centre for information with staff who have communication skills backed up with communication support technology. Weston Super Mare College has run successful open days with language and communication support for deaf and hard of hearing adults
- having deaf and hard of hearing staff and current or ex-students at recruitment events. The City Lit has found this very helpful for potential deaf or hard of hearing students for discrete and general courses.

The style and type of building of many larger educational institutions can be intimidating for deaf or hard of hearing adults coming back to study after a long time, and often it is more appropriate for a provider to run some discrete provision for deaf or hard of hearing adults and some general provision with support in environments which might be more familiar and less threatening, for example in community centres or in local voluntary deaf organisations and centres. Courses which might be run initially in the community with some later sessions in a further education college or university can help students become more familiar with larger institutions and more comfortable in more formal institutional environments. Courses which bridge institutions in this way can help deaf and hard of hearing adults progress to more advanced educational opportunities in the future in other institutions.

As with any provision for adults the timing of courses needs as far as possible to fit in with adults' other commitments and responsibilities, such as picking up children from school. The length of courses and particularly the length of classes need to be informed by the particular needs of deaf or hard of hearing adults. For example if a deaf student is relying on a British Sign Language interpreter the interpreters should change every half hour or have a break. In lipreading it is important that there are short breaks every half hour or so in the class. Interpreting, lipreading and following an interpreter are extremely tiring and require complete concentration. It would be better generally for classes to be shorter in length for the same reason, for example two rather than four hours. Attention to timing of courses in these ways can prevent providers inadvertently creating another barrier to the participation of deaf and hard of hearing adults.

Providers need also to protect time for deaf and hard of hearing students to have access to additional tutorial support if required, time for any special communication aids to be set up in the teaching room, for example a loop, and a short time before a class starts and possibly after a class finishes for any discussion needed with the deaf or hard of hearing student(s), the tutor and the interpreter or communicator.

Careful thought about time and planning by providers can ensure that learning opportunities are genuinely accessible and of good quality for deaf and hard of hearing adults, and that time and timing are not barriers to participation.

Costs

Fees can be a deterrent for any adult student, especially those on low incomes. Some deaf and hard of hearing adults are unemployed or employed in poorly paid jobs, so fees can be a critical barrier to participation if they are too high. As far as possible there should be no or low fees for discrete courses for deaf or hard of hearing adults, and any fee remission schemes should include deaf and hard of hearing adults as a category of people to benefit.

Deaf and hard of hearing adults may incur additional costs compared with hearing students, for example it they need a tape recorder or a radio microphone. As far as possible equipment to help communication and human aids to communication should be provided free, so that the cost of these essential support facilities is not a barrier.

Unsuitable admissions

Admissions procedures should be suitable for deaf and hard of hearing adults, with language and communication support built in as required. A hard of hearing person is more likely to perform well in interview if communication methods have been sorted out prior to the interview. Discussing communication needs can be a sensitive issue for a hard of hearing person. They may be reluctant to reveal their hearing loss in case they are discriminated against.

> *'I didn't tell them I was hard of hearing, as I thought they would not take me; I even covered up my hearing aid by wearing my hair down instead of up. I can speak quite well and I managed as best I could. In the end, though, I missed something and I had to own up. One of them talked badly after that but otherwise we managed' (mature student).*

Creating the right environment for a 'disclosure' of deafness is important, for example by asking the candidate if there are any practical arrangements which would help them in the interview, and checking everything is alright before the interview starts. These kinds of questions give someone who is deaf or hard of hearing the chance to say what would be helpful, such as members of the panel not sitting with their back to a window, which makes lipreading very difficult.

Criteria for admissions to courses need to be reviewed to ensure that they do not inadvertently create hurdles for deaf or hard of hearing applicants. For example, a requirement for work experience may be more suitable if it was broadened to include voluntary as well as paid work. Many deaf adults have had experience of teaching British Sign Language or have participated in deaf voluntary organisations but may not have been able to secure paid work. English language skills may be an implicit criteria which a deaf British Sign Language user may find it difficult to demonstrate, yet with language and literacy support they could be highly suitable students for the course.

Assessment of prior learing to enable a person to enter a programme with advanced standing can offer deaf and hard of hearing people the opportunity to demonstrate skills and competences they have gained through experience. This can be especially important, as many will not have had chance to gain qualifications in the past because of limited access to qualification bearing courses, for example in deaf schools. Again it is important that language and communication support are available to ensure that a person's learning can be assessed effectively.

Mobility, childcare and other possible barriers

As with all adult learning opportunities it is important to make sure that programmes are geographically accessible through, for example, use of outreach venues close to public transport routes. In some parts of the country deaf and hard of hearing students may be eligible for travel passes. Providers can make sure that information about any such travel schemes, usually available from local authorities, is passed on to potential students. Individual deaf or hard of hearing adults may find there are other barriers to their participation. Discussions during guidance or admissions interviews can cover any particular difficulties for individuals, and as far as possible the provider can try and respond by helping to resolve practical issues such as childcare so that the person can join the programme.

Barriers relating to background, past experiences and views of self

In addition to the wide range of practical barriers to participation for deaf and hard of hearing adults there are also many other aspects of people's circumstances and past experiences which can act as powerful, if sometimes less immediately apparent, barriers to participation.

Deaf education has sometimes not provided a sound basis for pupils feeling confident as learners, and has not instilled a keenness to continue learning and achieving as students after school. Deaf adults who as children had their hands restrained to prevent them signing in school often have very negative views of hearing education.

'I never really learnt much at school, only what my parents helped me with at home. At school we weren't allowed to sign, we had to put our hands behind our backs and try and speak. I could not understand the things the teachers said and I know now that my speech isn't very clear, although they told me it was at school. When I first went into a shop by myself after school the assistants laughed when I spoke, so after that I used sign language or wrote things down' (a deaf man now working as a baker).

'I was doing A-level sociology and we had to travel to another school to do it. Everytime the teacher said "it's time to go and get the bus", I missed her saying it and the two boys doing sociology always left without me, so I never caught the bus in time. That's only the information from teachers outside the subject, I don't know how much I missed actually in my classes' (a 25-year-old woman who lost her hearing at 16 after meningitis).

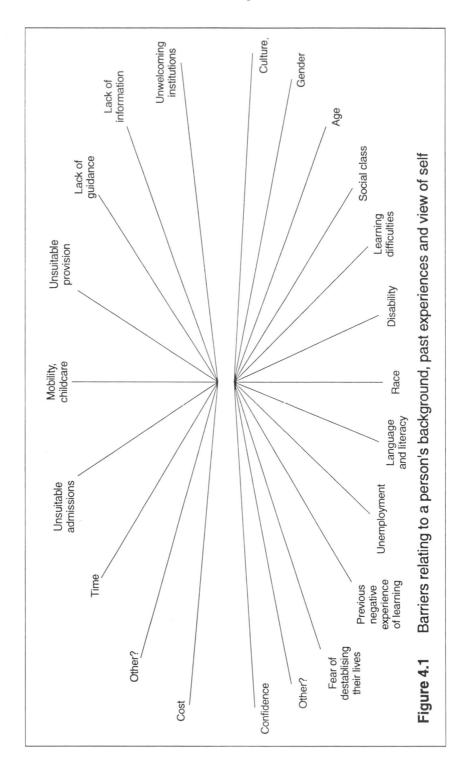

Figure 4.1   Barriers relating to a person's background, past experiences and view of self

'I was in a hearing school but even though I could lipread well and speak well I could never keep up. I know I wasn't doing as well as I should have done and I left school as soon as I could' (a hard of hearing woman working in a factory).

Many deaf or hard of hearing adults' negative experiences in education at school, college or later in adult education are a result of tutors' poor communication skills and deaf or hard of people's worries about communication:

'I joined an art class but the tutor kept standing behind me talking about the painting while looking at it and pointing. I asked him not to, but he always forgot' (a hard of hearing man in his sixties).

'I would never go to a class with hearing people because I would feel too embarrassed about my English. I would feel too stupid' (a Deaf women in her thirties who uses British Sign Language).

'I couldn't follow what was going on even though I read a lot in between and tried to keep up. I lost all confidence in myself. I finished the course but I never really enjoyed it and I never joined in with the group' (a local history student who is hard of hearing).

'I was used to being spoken to carefully and slowly at my school. It was a shock to find myself in an ordinary evening class where the teacher didn't bother' (a young man with partial hearing).

Some Deaf adults who use British Sign Language have poor literacy skills and left school not able to read very well in their second language, English. This also deters many deaf adults from considering adult education.

'I can't read complicated English and I'm ashamed of my writing – they tell me it's all wrong. A lot of Deaf people are like me, mostly I don't have to do much reading but sometimes I have to write things like to ask the way from a hearing person. I feel embarrassed' (a Deaf women who uses British Sign Language and works as a school cook).

Lack of confidence, previous bad experiences and poor levels of attainment in education and poor literacy skills can lead to many deaf or hard of hearing adults feeling that 'education is not for people like me'.

'I wouldn't feel I could go along to a college and knock on the door and ask to go in. They wouldn't want people like me. It's for hearing people, really, isn't it, all that?' (a Deaf man).

Many deaf and hard of hearing adults feel that they 'failed' to understand and keep up in school or other classes and they are clear that they do not want to repeat the experience of failure.

These issues need to be addressed by adult learning providers. Providers can convey clear messages at all stages that their provision is for deaf and hard of hearing adults, that there is language and communication support, that you do not need qualifications, that it is for people who feel they did not get on at school, that there is help with writing and/or that you do not need skills in writing, etc. Publicity which is accessible, discussion with individuals, presentations by deaf or hard of hearing people at open day or visits to deaf centres can all address the kinds of concerns that deaf and hard of hearing adults may have, so that they are more likely to feel 'this course is different – this course could be for people like me'.

Deaf and hard of hearing people are not a homogeneous group. They have different kinds of backgrounds which combine with deafness or partial loss of hearing to shape their views of themselves: their material circumstances, their experience of discrimination. These variables have often determined the opportunities available to them in the past.

A combination of disadvantages such as low income and deafness may compound difficulties; for example, a deaf or hard of hearing person on a low income is likely to live in poor housing, cannot afford many basic necessities and probably has no spare money at all for educational and training opportunities. It is also true that being deaf of itself can create other disadvantages; for example, deaf or hard of hearing people are more likely than hearing people to meet with discrimination in the labour market. Employers often judge them as unsuitable employees because they are seen to communicate in different ways from hearing people and need extra facilities and support which might be expensive for the employer. Unemployment or low level employment then combines with deafness to make education seem out of reach.

'Deaf people can't reach the same level as hearing people. We'll never advance, education does not prepare us so we cannot get good jobs. We only get jobs which allow us to feed ourselves, but no more than that ' (a respondent in a study of European deaf people: Jones and Pullen, 1990).

Deaf or hard of hearing adults from black or other ethnic and linguistic minorities may meet discrimination on two counts, their 'race' and their deafness. They are likely to be perceived in stereotypical ways such as 'stupid' or impossible to communicate with, which closes off opportunities and access to services as well as being undermining and potentially damaging to the person's dignity and self-esteem.

Adult education providers need to take into account these influences and make sure that the institution does not discriminate on the basis of deafness or any other grounds. It is important that they convey the institution's commitment to offering genuine equal opportunities to deaf and hard of hearing people from all backgrounds and that there is provision and support tailored to particular groups of deaf or hard of hearing adults, for example discrete courses for deaf or hard of hearing women, or community language support for black or ethnic minority deaf or hard of hearing students whose first language is not English or British Sign Language.

Barriers during a programme of study

The critical barriers of language and communication and ways of making sure suitable methods of communication, language and literacy support are part of any provision for deaf or hard of hearing adults are addressed in detail in Chapters 2, 3, 5 and 6. Literacy support may be needed by some deaf or hard of hearing adults. Discrete adult basic education provision and literacy skills does not prevent deaf or hard of hearing adults from participating in programmes.

Adults who have had negative past experience in education can benefit greatly from being able to 'unpack' that experience. It can help adults to discard any feelings they may still harbour of personal failure, and help them recognise that educational providers in the past may in fact have failed them by not providing suitable opportunities or support.

Sharing feelings of past negative educational experiences with other students who may also feel they have 'failed' also helps by proving that 'it's not only me': many other people have had bad experiences too and institutions have some responsibility for these experiences. In discrete classes for deaf or hard of hearing adults, or on courses designed specifically for people who have benefited least in the past from education, such as Access or Return to Learn courses, these discussions about past educational experiences can be a valuable part of an induction period or of the programme itself. If deaf or hard of hearing adults are joining other classes, guidance interviews or tutorials are probably best for discussing past educational experiences. Issues and feelings arising from students' schooling and other educational experiences can be an invaluable guide to course tutors. They can alert them to any concerns students have and the kinds of teaching and learning strategies which have, or have not, worked for them in the past. The tutor can then build on what was successful previously and avoid approaches that did not work.

Hearing tutors are likely to feel concerned about their competence to meet the needs of deaf or hard of hearing adults on discrete courses or other courses. They will be keen to ensure that deaf or hard of hearing students are successful in their studies, and that they are working alongside hearing students, that they feel full members of the group and that deaf, hard of hearing and hearing students communicate well with each other and with the tutor, and that they all effectively use interpreters or communicators in the group.

Deaf or hard of hearing students often bring distinct advantages and benefits to the learning group:

'I was worried beforehand, but in fact having hearing Deaf students helped my teaching really. I had to prepare more in advance and have very clear outlines for each session' (tutor on an integrated course).

'In the end it was easier with the deaf student in the group because it stopped people interrupting. Also I had never spoken directly to the deaf student until one day the interpreter went to make a phone call and then I did. The trouble with there being an interpreter there is that you go through them all the time. We managed to communicate.'

Learning contracts can help make clear what the institution will provide for the deaf or hard of hearing student, and also what the student expects of the provider, what they want to achieve and how they will aim to do this. The learning contract can include very practical concerns, such as whose responsibility it is to book and set up the portable loop system; an agreement about when the tutor, student and interpreter will meet before each class and discuss what the class will include; an agreement about continuity of interpreters, guaranteeing that the same interpreter will be employed for each class, etc. Learning contracts can clarify and resolve issues which otherwise may emerge as difficulties later on. Parkwood College in Sheffield has drawn up learning contracts for deaf and hard of hearing students and found them effective.

Barriers at the point of exit from a programme

Deaf or hard of hearing adults can find progression to more advanced education or training or employment more difficult than hearing people. Lack of understanding and awareness of deafness or discrimination on the part of admissions tutors or employers often work against them.

Adult education providers need to ensure as far as possible that steps are taken to ease the transition to the 'next phase' for deaf and hard of hearing students. Guidance staff, careers advisers and course tutors play especially important roles in discussing options for progression. They are also well placed to discuss how best to tackle completing application forms, going for interviews, etc. and how and at what point the student wants to inform employers or other tutors about their deafness and any kinds of support or facilities they might need. Any references given or advocacy interventions by adult education providers should be in consultation or partnership with the deaf or hard of hearing student. In particular, there needs to be agreement on how information relating to the student's deafness is conveyed to others. It is vital that the student feels comfortable with the way they present themselves to others and that they can manage their deafness with confidence when they move to another course or into work.

Collaborating to overcome barriers

Many of the barriers and ways of overcoming them at all stages of the learning process can be addressed by an individual adult education provider. However, collaboration and co-working with other agencies can often lead to more effective and comprehensive dismantling of barriers.

Collaboration to help overcome barriers to participation

The discrete Nursery Nurses Examination Board Certificate course for Deaf students at Basford Hall College, Nottingham was set up because of a clear demand from the local Deaf community and because of demands from schools for qualified nursery nurses to work with deaf children in schools and in home–school liaison work. Both groups helped identify the kind of course needed and how it should be organised. Funding for the course came from several different agencies, none of whom could have funded the course independently. The English for Speakers of other Languages service and the hearing impaired support service from Basford College provided language and communication support for students. The Nottingham and Nottinghamshire Society for the Deaf provided interpreters. Derby College for the Deaf agreed to provide residential places and minibus transport for some students. The North British Housing Association agreed to provide flats for other students. Local Deaf agencies and centres helped to publicise the course and to encourage deaf people to apply for places. Basford Hall College provided tutors and teaching accommodation and took on responsibility for organising and running the course.

5
Learning Opportunities and Teaching and Learning Strategies

Identifying needs

Extending the range

Adult basic education

Information technology

Health promotion

Courses for black and other ethnic minority adults

Counselling

Performing and visual arts

Courses for women

Return to learn

Qualification bearing courses

Work-based training and learning

General adult education

Deaf studies

Suitable teaching and learning strategies

'I have found the perfect class for someone who is hard of hearing. I just stand behind the person in front of me and watch – I do everything they do. I don't have to worry about what the teacher is saying, I just enjoy myself. I wish all classes were like that.'

This middle-aged keep fit student felt liberated by finding a class where she could join in easily. She described her 'find' to the rest of her lipreading class. It is often difficult for adults who are deaf or hard of hearing join and benefit from a class. Although a visual class may sometimes be easier, it is only rarely a solution.

NIACE's wide-ranging survey of educational provision for deaf and hard of hearing adults (see Appendix 1) showed clearly that the curriculum offer for deaf and hard of hearing adults is generally narrow. The main findings of the survey are:

- that provision for Deaf adults using British Sign Language is mainly in the areas of adult basic education and information technology (discrete courses for Deaf adults using British Sign Language)
- on some qualification bearing courses there is support for Deaf people using British Sign Language (general courses with specialist support for Deaf adults using British Sign Language)
- lipreading is the main form of course provision for adults who are hard of hearing (discrete courses for hard of hearing adults)
- British Sign Language classes are predominantly taken up by hearing adults, although providers often see them as mainstay provision for Deaf adults (general courses for hearing adults)
- British Sign Language courses are not usually a form of direct provision for Deaf adults, but are of indirect benefit to them by providing a basis for language and communication.

Literacy, language and communication skills and information technology are all vitally important subject areas, but clearly they are not adequate as the total curriculum offer for deaf and hard of hearing adults. They need to be complemented by a wide range of other learning opportunities.

'The range of subjects a deaf person is allowed to follow is severely limited, not because of our ability, but because education organisers won't allow us to take part. I have lost count of the number of courses I have been turned down for because they haven't got the equipment or trained people to help you take part' (middle-aged Deaf woman from South Wales commenting on the situation).

On two counts deaf and hard of hearing adults are denied access to the same curriculum range as hearing people: firstly because discrete courses specifically for them are from an extremely restricted range, and secondly because participation in general learning opportunities is, in most cases, impossible. Extending the discrete curriculum and extending general course support arrangements for deaf and hard of hearing adults are key issues which need to be addressed by providers and policy-makers.

As well as demonstrating the limitations of provision for deaf and hard of hearing adults the NIACE survey also gives some examples of practice which can be used to improve and develop educational opportunities for deaf and hard of hearing adults. It shows that there are scattered examples of excellent and innovative discrete courses for deaf and hard of hearing adults, along with practical and imaginative kinds of support in general classes. Although these are the exception, and are usually insecurely resourced, they do prove that good provision is offered and that a better range of opportunities can be made available. They provide illustrations of good practice which can be copied and adopted.

The kinds of good quality provision found fall into three main groupings which are particularly significant because of a focus on:

- curriculum: both content and teaching and learning approaches (see this chapter)
- styles and settings (Chapter 6)
- language and communication and ways of facilitating learning (Chapter 7).

In the following sections various aspects of the curriculum for deaf and hard of hearing adults are discussed under the broad headings of ident- ifying the needs of deaf and hard of hearing adults and extending the range of subjects available.

Identifying needs

The curriculum of any programme for deaf or hard of hearing adults should address the language and communication needs of the learners as a central concern. Because providers generally know relatively little about deaf or hard of hearing adults' expectations, learning needs and requirements, care should be taken to involve them in course planning and development at all stages of the learning programme (before, during and after) to help determine the subject area(s), the kinds of language and communication support needed and the teaching and learning strategies which will be most suitable.

Extending the range of subjects available

Within the existing fairly narrow curriculum offer specifically for deaf and hard of hearing adults it is possible to ensure that these discrete courses are suitable for all groups of learners. There should, for example, be provision for Deaf people who use British Sign Language and who want to improve their signing skills or gain a qualification in British Sign

Language, and adult basic education provision specifically for hard of hearing adults.

A large range of subject areas was identified in the NIACE survey, although there were very few examples of the different types of courses. The subjects offered included:

- adult basic education
- information technology
- health promotion
- courses for black and other ethnic minority adults
- counselling
- performing arts
- courses for women
- return to learn and access courses
- qualification bearing vocational courses and other accredited courses
- work-based training and learning
- general adult education
- Deaf studies.

The existence of this range of provision across Britain shows the tremendous potential there is for improving the suitability and range of curriculum available for deaf and hard of hearing adults. Descriptions of the characteristics of each type of course are given below with some illustrative case studies of practice from different parts of Britain.

Adult basic education

Nearly all literacy courses reported to the NIACE survey were discrete courses for Deaf people who use British Sign Language. There is a strong demand and need for improved literacy skills amongst Deaf adults, in the form of courses which are an end in themselves and also a means of enabling them to move on to other courses. The average reading age of Deaf school leavers in the 1970s was only eight and three-quarters (Conrad, 1978). When mixing in a hearing world deaf people who do not speak have severe difficulty communicating unless they can write and read notes. Literacy is also vital for access to subtitles on television and films, as well as all the print media. Without good literacy skills, access to educational opportunities as an adult is severely restricted, compounding previous educational disadvantage.

'I have a place on a computer HND course, but my English always lets me down. I have failed the GCSE twice now and they will not keep my place open much longer' (a Deaf man in his twenties in the Midlands).

'I tried to do the 7307 teacher training course but I had problems with the English. I had to drop out in the end' (an experienced British Sign Language tutor in the North of England).

The survey found some examples of adult basic education programmes and materials being designed specifically for, or adapted for, deaf and hard of hearing adults.

Improving English

(Derby College of Further Education, Wilmorton, Derby Unit for Deaf Students)

This unit provides a range of adult basic education courses as well as drop-in basic skills workshops. There are also drop-in English classes and life skills groups.

The English class is staffed with a communicator (British Sign Language), a hearing lecturer (with sign-supported English skills) and an English teacher (hearing). Classes run in the day and evening and on average 12 students attend each session, with some 50 students registered, half aged 19 and over.

'I go to the English workshops. I have been to dressmaking, cooking and painting evening classes but found them hard to follow, although I did finish them. I feel I would have learned more with a communicator in these classes. In the English workshop at the College I can ask questions, which I've never been able to do in classes before' (a 66-year-old Deaf woman who is a sign language tutor and is also studying English GCSE).

'I'm doing BTEC in computer studies but I've failed English GCSE twice. At home the languages spoken are Urdu, Punjabi, Arabic, French and English. My mother is now also learning sign language so we can communicate better. I use speech and lipreading as well as some sign language. I desperately need more English support because in the English GCSE I could not even fully understand the questions. I find the College's English

classes helpful but I will still need more support for the
examinations' (a Deaf student).

Literacy for moving on

(The Two-Can Resources Unit, Derbyshire County Council)

The Two-Can Resources Unit is based on the idea that two people
working together can achieve greater literacy. The Unit has both Deaf
tutors and communicators. The Unit aims to act as a transitional
provider between Deaf centres and adult education, giving people
access to Derbyshire's community education programmes. English
is taught as a second language and the Unit has produced a series of
publications and worksheets for Deaf people, for example 'Labell-
ling', which encourages students to build up their vocabulary by
labelling pictures, 'Letter Writing' and 'The Past Tense', to help
students understand and practice the simple past tense.

Integrated literacy developments

(Chesterfield College of Arts and Technology)

The College runs an adult basic education programme in conjunction
with the Derbyshire Hearing Impaired Support Service. Recently
student numbers have declined, due in part to the loss of funding for
taxi transport for the rural catchment area, and also, so the tutor
thought, because some students felt embarrassed attending a literacy
class. A new scheme, 'Personal Safety', supported by the police and
other outside speakers, intends to integrate literacy development and
support into the programme to help overcome this embarrassment
and to attract deaf adults who would not come to literacy classes or
workshops.

Information technology

Information technology courses were mainly discrete courses for Deaf
adults who use sign language. Computing and information technology
have great potential for Deaf and hard of hearing adults because they
operate using visual input and output. Computers can also give access to

learning in just about all other subject areas, for example book-keeping, keyboard skills and sciences, through a wide range of educational software, interactive tutorial packages and information storage systems. Information technology can also provide access for deaf and hard of hearing adults to a wide range of services which can help their everyday life as well as their learning, for example use of videophones. There are a few specialist technology research and development centres which specialise in adapting or developing new information technology systems and applications for deaf and hard of hearing people, for example Reading University's Deaf Enterprise Trust and Development Centre on Deafness, and Cheshire Deaf Society's technology initiative. Recent technological developments for deaf and hard of hearing people have included a computerised bulletin board and videophones in certain libraries in rural areas with computer link-ups to enable sign language and lipreading to be used (although this is difficult because the videophones have very small screens).

Successful computer courses

- residential computer courses at Bristol University's Continuing Education Department with Deaf tutors
- 'Signing for Skills', a computing and office skills course taught using sign language at South Bristol and Soundwell Colleges in Bristol
- computing skills for deaf people at various centres, including Kent University's Department of Continuing Education, The City Lit and Camden Local Education Authority
- A word processing course at Sutton College of Liberal Arts has offered a deaf student a volunteer co-student who acts as a link for her between both the tutor and the other students and helps with communication. This is an interim measure to enable the deaf student to do the course until funding for a communicator is identified.

Health promotion

Health promotion has proved one of the most successful areas of development in adult education, especially in the voluntary sector and in informal learning groups within the Deaf community. It has developed mainly for Deaf adults who use British Sign Language.

Promoting health for Deaf adults

The British Deaf Health Promotion Service began only in 1993 but has produced (in conjunction with Glaxo Holdings plc) a *Healthy Living Guide* for older Deaf people who use British Sign Language, using graphics and plain English for accessibility. Deaf link workers are used to support the dissemination of the guide.

Aids education

Since 1987 the Aids Ahead initiative has raised awareness within the Deaf community and for those who are hard of hearing through:

- producing information in British Sign Language
- training Deaf health promotion workers
- training Deaf counsellors
- training interpreters in this specialist area both in oral and sign language.

Deaf women's health

The Deaf Women's Health Project based in Manchester and funded by the Department of Health's Opportunities for Volunteering works in the area of access to information for Deaf women so that they can make their own decisions about their health. The project has:

- used Deaf interviewers to gather information about Deaf women's health experiences and find out what information they would like to have
- trained Deaf women volunteers to offer support and information to other Deaf women and to involve them in evaluating existing health materials
- set up a network of trained Deaf support workers to be available for Deaf women with serious health problems
- researched and produced video information tapes in British Sign Language.

Comments from women in the project reveal how important it is:

'Many Deaf people do not realise that cancer can be cured if it is caught early enough. Many friends deserted me because they thought my cancer was catching. When I was in hospital all the other patients had cancer and they could talk to one another. I could not share my anxieties. I felt alone and upset.'

'Like most Deaf people I did not get enough information. I did not know I might have a mastectomy until half an hour before I went into the operating theatre. No one had mentioned the possibility of cancer. I was given a leaflet about chemotherapy and radio therapy but I did not fully understand it. I can read – what happens to Deaf people who can't?'

The project was linked with other organisations both locally and nationally on Deaf women's health issues and joint initiatives have included:

- training Deaf women health education volunteers in conjunction with BACUP and Cancer Link in the North West region and in Bristol and Scotland
- running women's health courses for Deaf women jointly with the Workers' Educational Association (WEA) in Manchester and Bristol.

The project has also run several new courses for Deaf women including:

- confidence building
- back to work/training
- 'Look after your heart' (A Deaf woman project worker trained as a tutor for 'Look after your heart' courses at Salford General hospital along with 16 hearing participants. An interpreter was provided)
- specialist health interpreter training courses, including a residential course in Wales on 'HIV/Aids and sexuality: issues for interpreters'.

Successful health promotion initiatives seem to have certain key characteristics:

- using good quality, up to date materials adapted for users of British Sign Language, either by using sign language or plain English with graphics or video
- training Deaf and hard of hearing counsellors and tutors
- involving Deaf and hard of hearing people at every stage of material development or adaptation
- employing Deaf and hard of hearing tutors
- providing specialist health promotion training courses for British Sign Language and oral interpreters.

Courses for black and other ethnic minority adults

There are some 97,000 Deaf black and other ethnic minority people in Britain (Royal Association of the Deaf, 1991). Generally, they do not get access to the same services and opportunities as white Deaf people. Several courses for black and other ethnic minority Deaf people were reported to the NIACE survey. At the Centre for Deaf People in Leicester an Asian Deaf woman social worker collected information about the needs of Asian Deaf people and then set up a Deaf Asian Women's Group. Some of the group members worked using British Sign Language, but some of the women had little sign language and were 'language-less'. Language and communication skills work with these women led on to literacy work. An Asian men's group was then also set up. Newham Community College and Hackney Adult Education Institute are also involved in Asian Deaf women's groups.

There is a growing demand for more black and other ethnic minority interpreters, especially interpreters with other community language skills. Black Deaf groups and Asian women's groups have revealed the double dominance of a hearing and white culture. Cross-cultural communication is essential in order to have more equal relations across Deaf and hearing and black and white communities. There are a few courses which are designed to address cross-cultural issues for black deaf adults. For example The City Lit runs a New Start course for deaf people who have recently moved to the UK and may be users of another sign language, and some of the Asian Deaf groups are developing British Sign Language for users of other sign languages.

Counselling

Counselling has been a growth area, partly as a result of health promotion initiatives and Health Authorities working to improve their services for deaf and hard of hearing people. In the past deaf people using counselling services have had to cope with an 'intruder' in the counselling process: an interpreter. Fears about confidentiality and embarrassment at the presence of a third party prevented many Deaf people who use British Sign Language from even thinking about counselling. There was a recognised need for trained deaf and hard of hearing counsellors. Counselling training is provided both through specialist counselling courses and as part of other training courses.

Counselling courses

- the Springfield Hospital, London and the Westminster Pastoral Foundation has run two-year, half-day a week certificated Counselling Skills and Attitudes for Deaf Trainees courses, and Counselling Diploma courses. Tutors and interpreters are provided
- Manchester University Department of Extra Mural Studies offers a counselling course for users of British Sign Language run by a deaf psychologist. It began as a one-off 10-week basic counselling course, and is now running for the third time because of demand
- a health care assistant training course run by Springfield Hospital, London, Westminster Pastoral Foundation, St George's Hospital and Queen Mary's Roehampton School of Nursing
- a mental health course to prepare deaf nursing staff to move on to take the mental nursing qualification. This course is seeking to offer a National Vocational Qualification so that deaf staff gain nationally recognised accreditation.

The number of voluntary and paid jobs for deaf and hard of hearing adults as counsellors or as workers where counselling skills are very important is increasing. For example RELATE employs a hard of hearing counsellor, *See Hear*, the BBC/Royal National Institute for Deaf People magazine, has a deaf 'agony aunt' and counselling skills are increasingly required for the full range of caring professions.

Performing and visual arts

The visual arts, and in particular photography, can offer deaf and hard of hearing adults opportunities to develop their skills and talents with fewer difficulties than many other subjects which rely more on oracy and verbal communication. Surprisingly, there seemed to be relatively few examples of discrete photography courses for deaf adults.

Photography courses

- a taster course run by Soundwell College, Bristol for adults who are hard of hearing has managed to overcome difficulties of lipreading in the darkroom by using flashlights shining on the face of the person speaking
- Pimlico Arts and Media, an independent company, runs photography courses for deaf people
- the Museum of the Moving Image and SHAPE, London run a practical evening class and a seminar for Deaf adults on animation using stop-frame video.

There were several discrete video skills course and television courses. Videos were also used to assist communication for deaf and hard of hearing students and were used for assessing students on courses. As with adult basic education provision, students learn video skills for their own value and interest and/or as a means of enabling the students to move on and participate more effectively in other courses.

Video skills and television courses

- video skills courses for deaf and hard of hearing adults are run at Liverpool Community College by the London Deaf Access Project and by Hammersmith Action for Disability. The latter is a 20-week course taught by a Deaf tutor using British Sign Language with an interpreter providing voice-over for the one partially hearing student. The course offers London Open College Federation accreditation
- Berkshire Education Authority runs a technology course which includes interactive videos for deaf people
- Merseyside Centre for the Deaf runs a City and Guilds Video Production course taught by two Deaf British Sign Language users. An independent Deaf video production company, 'Silent View', was formed by trainees on the course
- a north-east media training course is provided by Tyne Tees Television. It provides training for deaf television and film technicians and includes work placements at Tyne Tees. Six camera technicians who completed the course two years ago formed their

own production company 'Deaf Owl', which has made programmes for television, industry and public services.

Several performing arts courses have been developed successfully, for example at The City Lit, by Mid Glamorgan County Council and at Reading University, where there is a two-year Diploma in Theatre of the Deaf course. SHAPE has done a great deal to further Deaf arts and has run several successful drama courses. Signed poetry and songs are also taught, and signed dance is being developed as a discipline. Dorothy Miles was the first British Deaf poet to reach a wider audience and encourage drama and song for Deaf people, and she contributed to educational opportunities for deaf and hard of hearing adults in the arts.

Courses for women

Although women constitute some 75 per cent of the adult education enrolments nationally (Sargant, 1991), there are no statistics about the participation of deaf and hard of hearing women. There are, however, some deaf women's courses developing, but much more slowly than hearing women's courses. Merseyside Centre for the Deaf and Liverpool Community College run Return to Work schemes for women. The Centre for Deaf People in Leicester runs a Deaf Asian Women's Group and a Deaf Young Women's Group. A deaf women's discussion group at Chesterfield College now runs its own cookery classes, and has recently opened these sessions to men. (See the earlier section on health promotion for various other Deaf women's health projects.) Assertion training for deaf and hard of hearing women is growing in popularity and is challenging the feeling some women have that 'expressing your own needs' is in some sense impolite.

Assertion training for deaf women

Audiovisual Services in Carlisle began assertion training courses for deaf women in the mid 1980s in response to requests from deaf women tutors on British Sign Language courses who felt that they wanted to become more assertive. Courses are now run across the country, with both deaf and hearing tutors. A video in British Sign Language adapting assertion training material for deaf women was made recently and increasingly other resource materials are being developed. Issues specific to deaf participants include ways of saying 'no' which are culturally acceptable to deaf people using British Sign Language, using facial expressions and placement assertively and feeling confident that 'I have a right to make a mistake', which is especially important for deaf and hard of hearing people, as mis-understandings in communication with hearing people are common.

Assertion training for hard of hearing women

Assertion training is part of the 'Living with hearing loss' course run by Bristol University's Department of Continuing Education. Part of the course looks at hearing tactics. For example, a hard of hearing person may want to sit in a certain place at a meeting in order to be able to lipread as well as possible and so might need others to move seats and change their behaviour, perhaps by speaking more slowly or not covering their mouth, and to ask with confidence, and as far as possible without creating tension. Hearing tactics between hearing and hard of hearing partners or colleagues are also explored on the course.

Return to learn and access courses

Compared with provision for hearing adults, and in particular hearing women, return to learn and access courses for deaf and hard of hearing adults are hugely underdeveloped, despite a general commitment by policy-makers to opportunities for progression and certification for adults with disabilities or learning difficulties, including deaf and hard of hearing adults, who have often missed out on education in school.

Return to learn courses

- the Workers' Educational Association in West Mercia adapted their Second Chance materials for use with deaf adults who are users of British Sign Language. Two deaf tutors were employed to adapt the materials and teach the groups, and there was also an interpreter for the course
- The City Lit, the Leap Centre in Durham and Liverpool Com-munity College run return to learn courses for deaf adults. The Liverpool course is for women

- the number of 'access to the professions' courses is slowly growing. These support deaf workers in new work roles, and also aim to attract others into various professions. The City Lit runs a course for deaf workers in education which is aimed at those working or hoping to work in deaf education, but are not qualified teachers. It is designed for British Sign Language users who have a commitment to bilingual education for deaf children and adults and who have sufficient competence in the English language (spoken or written), as well as an awareness of current issues in the deaf community. It runs one day a week for 30 weeks and aims to cover both theory and practice in education, and enable participants to develop teaching skills so that they can move on to employment in various capacities in education or more advanced professional training
- Leeds Metropolitan University runs a course on professional development skills for deaf people working in health and social care.

Qualification bearing vocational and other accredited courses

National Vocational Qualifications (NVQs) provide a competence-based accreditation framework which should be accessible to deaf and hard of hearing adults because they are designed to assess only a person's competence, irrespective of gender, race, disability, past qualifications, etc. The possibility of using Assessment of Prior Learning to count towards NVQs also means that deaf and hard of hearing adults' past experience rather than their qualifications or attendance on courses can be used to gain vocational qualifications. Many deaf and hard of hearing adults have few formal qualifications but much experience and well-developed skills. A great deal of liaison and negotiation with Awarding Bodies by organisations such as Skill: the National Bureau for Students with Disabilities has led to a number of suggested changes in standards and assessment requirements. For example, within the NVQ in Business Administration the unit which covers voice telephone skills and systems in offices can be adapted for text telephones or Typetalk systems. Verbal skills are replaced by communication skills so that the qualification does not discriminate against deaf and hard of hearing adults. The City and Guilds Wordpower has been adapted for deaf and hard of hearing adults and there are also a number of new qualifications specifically for deaf and hard of hearing adults such as the RSA English for Hearing Impaired People. Open College Networks offer a nationally recognised accreditation framework which can be used to ensure access to credits for programmes across all curriculum areas and credits specifically designed for adults who are deaf or hard of hearing.

The qualifications for interpreter training are currently being examined to see if using the National Vocational Qualifications competence-based system would be suitable.

Many deaf and hard of hearing adults are keen to gain recognised qualifications to enhance their prospects in education, training and employment. Relatively minor adaptations can often make accreditation systems accessible to deaf and hard of hearing adults.

Work-based training and learning

Access to training in the workplace is usually very limited for deaf and hard of hearing adults because employers may think they would not want to attend, the information about courses may not reach them and there may not be suitable support available for them to participate.

> *'At work they didn't even bother to ask me if I wanted to go on training days. When I asked, they (the management) said that they thought it would be too "difficult". It is always going to be, if that's their attitude' (young deaf man).*

> *'I always sit and eat my sandwiches in the car at lunchtime. The others just talk among themselves so it's easier to sit out there. It does mean I miss a lot of what's going on, though' (deaf man working on a building site).*

The NIACE survey reveals many examples of opportunities for staff training for deaf and hard of hearing employees being made available, and provision of Deaf awareness courses for hearing employees.

Work-based training opportunities

Steven started working with J. Sainsbury plc as a trainee administration assistant and then moved to Homebase head office.

> *'When Steven arrived we used to write everything down for him. Then the company paid for a few of us to go to an adult education class and learn to sign. We didn't tell Steven and one day we just began signing' (technical manager).*

Steven commented that he was pleased and surprised. Steven also went on courses at The City Lit funded by the company to increase his skills. Steven now has qualifications in English, GCSEs in commerce and art and two RSA certificates in typing and computer studies. In this case linking with The City Lit specialist courses was the best way of meeting the individual employee's needs.

Some TECs have given support for deaf and hard of hearing employees to participate in staff training.

General adult education

A wide range of cultural, social, crafts, leisure, arts and fitness courses, etc. are available for hearing adults, yet there were few examples of these being offered specifically for hard of hearing or deaf adults, and few examples of support available to enable them to participate in general programmes. Most examples were in London or run by Deaf organisations.

Learning and leisure

The Isle of Wight Deaf Project runs a range of leisure courses and holidays including:

- storytelling workshops: 'capture and maintain the excitement of your audience with gestures that shout and characters that burst with energy using the techniques mastered by Deaf performers and theatre interpreters'
- silent weekend: a non-verbal weekend for those learning sign language
- family retreat
- sports.

The project also runs a number of activity holidays for young Deaf people encouraging independence, confidence, assertiveness and motivation.

Creative learning in Bristol

Bristol University's Department of Continuing Education has expanded its programme to include leisure classes for hard of hearing and deafened people. Courses include 'Relax with your hearing loss', a weekend course covering aromatherapy, foot massage, painting, printmaking, pottery and creative writing. It was taught by three hard of hearing and three hearing tutors. Students' comments on a creative writing residential weekend included:

'This course helped me to see the way people with a hearing impairment are too often on the receiving end of other people's ideas. My lack of hearing is not an end to the formation of original ideas, it just acts as a dampener to making further progress.'

'It was a great relief – the tutors didn't speak too fast, no one spoke with their hands over their mouths ... I went on a writing course before and I was treated as a bit of an idiot.'

'The course was important because people with hearing problems often can't compare their work with other people's because of communication problems. My confidence needed a big boost and it got it.'

'The photocopying of written material was important because it would have been hard work to listen/lipread well to all the inputs. It also gives you a chance to look back on the notes afterwards when you're at home.'

The creative writing course had 16 students all aged over 40 and ran with a hearing tutor, two notetakers and two lipspeakers. A hard of hearing outside speaker, who was an author, talked on publishing.

Activity-based classes such as sports, relaxation, crafts, etc. which are largely visual and based on demonstrations can be more accessible for deaf and hard of hearing adults, but they too can be problematic.

'I explained to the yoga tutor that I was hard of hearing and when she had the tape on I couldn't hear and if she spoke when we were relaxing with our eyes closed I couldn't lipread and I was lost. At first she was really helpful and we agreed I'd bring my Walkman and she would bring another copy of the tape. I

*could then listen to it at top volume. At the next class she'd
forgotten to bring the tape. I was so upset I actually cried. Then I
felt I was letting myself down, so I just walked out of the class.
The desolation was out of all proportion to the incident, really,
but it just seemed to bring back memories of all the other times
I'd been let down, when just a bit of effort would have helped.'*

*'Yes, I went to yoga but I had to give it up: lying down and
sticking my neck up to lipread was hard work. Relaxation it
wasn't! The trouble is for people like us, listening is not
relaxation, you're working. Yoga is a contradiction in terms.'*

At Soundwell College, Bristol a discrete yoga course for hard of hearing adults runs successfully. The tutor:

- always waits to demonstrate until she's finished speaking so that students are not trying to follow a movement and lipread at the same time
- explains how much time there will be to try a movement so that the students are free to concentrate on the yoga position without trying to listen or lipread at the same time
- tries to keep movements relying on closed eyes to a minimum, and when doing relaxation explains the sequence clearly and slowly beforehand
- tries to slow down and streamline the whole process so that there are no asides and chit-chat as students are working.

A swimming student who had to bung her ears with cotton wool and whose goggles misted up so that she could not lipread succeeded because the tutor waited until she was at the side and talked to her with the goggles off, and because it was one-to-one teaching. A riding student also felt that one-to-one teaching is best. When she tried to learn in a group it had not worked. The tutor had called to the group of riding students that they should divide into 'jumpers' and 'non-jumpers', but because the student did not hear the instruction she went with the jumpers and ended up hanging on to the horse as it careered over the jumps, losing a stirrup and then falling off. Sadly she had not been on a horse since because of this nightmare experience.

Deaf studies

There are an increasing number of Deaf heritage courses, and just as with women's studies courses and black studies courses they have been seen as essential for the cultural growth and development of the Deaf community. The Workers' Educational Association in West Mercia ran a Deaf reminiscence course using videos to record memories with a Deaf tutor. More resources suitable for Deaf studies are being produced (Jackson, 1990), which is assisting the further development of Deaf heritage work and the uncovering of Deaf people's hidden history. A Deaf Heritage Society has also been established.

Storytelling has developed alongside Deaf heritage as a way of recording Deaf history. Its narrative in British Sign Language is important and culturally distinct from spoken language storytelling. Derby College for the Deaf has run a very successful series of sign language storytelling courses.

'I love to watch a Deaf person telling a story. It makes me feel proud of my culture. It is the same as hearing people telling their children fairy stories or stories of when they were young' (a Deaf club member).

Suitable teaching and learning strategies

Extending the range of courses offered for deaf and hard of hearing adults, although vitally important, will not bring real benefits to deaf and hard of hearing people unless the teaching and learning strategies are suitable. How you learn is just as important as what you learn. Employing deaf and hard of hearing tutors brings many benefits to courses for deaf and hard of hearing adults through offering relative ease of communication and cultural understanding between students and tutors.

A number of guidelines for those working with deaf and hard of hearing people have been produced by various agencies. The key features of existing guidelines are outlined in Chapter 7.

Conclusion

Although the curriculum offer for deaf and hard of hearing adults is on the whole narrowly focused on adult basic education, information technology and lipreading, there is also a great deal of interesting and varied work in some parts of the country.

Improving the range of discrete and integrated courses and improving access to accreditation and progression are all central issues for those involved in adult learning to address. It is hoped that the examples of good practice described here can be used to assist policy-makers, managers and tutors to bring about a better and more varied curriculum for deaf and hard of hearing adults in the future.

6

Styles and Settings for Learning

Discrete or integrated courses?

Discrete courses

Integrated courses

Open and distance learning

Where deaf and hard of hearing people learn

The previous chapter explored ways in which the range of courses and approaches to teaching and learning could be developed to improve learning opportunities for deaf and hard of hearing adults. It is also vital that the best ways of organising and setting up learning opportunities are considered: discrete courses or integrated courses; open learning or taught groups; which type of provider is best placed to provide courses?

There are examples across the country of successful learning programmes for deaf and hard of hearing adults which have been set up in different ways, developing from the student group and their needs, the course content and the purpose of the course.

The language and communication arrangements used in provision for deaf and hard of hearing adults will influence the kind of provision it is possible to set up. For example if British Sign Language is used it may be preferable to set up a discrete course for deaf participants, but if English is used then integration is possible. If British Sign Language is the medium for teaching several options are possible (see Figure 6).

Discrete or integrated courses?

Increasingly, deaf students who use British Sign Language want discrete courses. These can be taught by deaf tutors who use British Sign Language because British Sign Language is their first language, part of their cultural identity and is the most efficient language in which they learn. Integration is sometimes seen as a dirty word by the Deaf community and is sometimes signed as 'oppression' by its Deaf opponents and referred to as genocidal because it suppresses sign language and Deaf culture. In some cases, the availability of specialist subject tutors and interpreters, resources and the

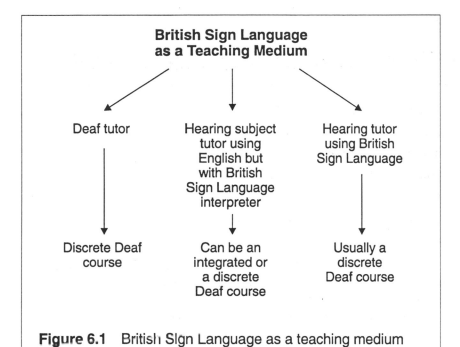

Figure 6.1 British Sign Language as a teaching medium

Discrete Courses

Advantages	Disadvantages	Issues
BSL or communication support throughout, therefore good access to information. Lack of embarassment about pace.	Narrow curriculum range.	

Integrated Courses

Advantages	Disadvantages	Issues
Wider curriculum range.	Poor access to information.	Language and communication support. Technology.
Contact with hearing students.	Being left out in group interaction.	Staff/student development.

Figure 6.2 Discrete and integrated courses

funding available may influence the final choice about how a course is run and the communication used.

'I have to pretend all the time that I can follow when I am with the hearing students' (Deaf NNEB student).

'I can express myself better in sign language' (Deaf student on an integrated A-level course).

'I felt happier with the Deaf students. I don't have to worry about communication and if I don't understand I can ask' (Deaf student on a discrete course).

If integrated courses are set up this can widen the curriculum choice for deaf and hard of hearing adults as long as there is adequate communication support to make mainstream courses accessible. Support may take the form of a sign language interpreter, notetaker or a lipspeaker.

Adults who are hard of hearing have usually lost some of their hearing later in life and so may find it easier to participate in integrated courses than deaf adults who use British Sign Language. However, hard of hearing adults are now beginning to ask for discrete courses, for similar reasons to the Deaf community.

Providers need to consider the advantages and disadvantages of different types of course, the language used as the teaching medium and the issues involved in each of the options.

Discrete courses

The recent NIACE survey of provision for deaf and hard of hearing adults (see Appendix 1) showed that some 31 educational institutions provided discrete courses for deaf adults. Much of the provision was made by Deaf societies or institutes and other voluntary organisations. Most discrete provision for deaf or hard of hearing adults was for British Sign Language users, with very little available for deaf people who use speech and lipreading rather than sign language.

Discrete courses for deaf adults

- Bridgewater College runs discrete computing courses, Bradford and Ilkley College runs a discrete youth work course, Preston College provides a discrete literacy course at the Deaf club and a discrete British Sign Language course at Whittingham Hospital

- a pioneering discrete NNEB course was set up at Basford Hall College, Nottingham which is taught in British Sign Language by a hearing and deaf tutor. There is a full-time interpreter and assessment is through a video of sign language answers and exam questions. Sign language and English are taught as part of the programme and the students are mainly British Sign Language users.

Discrete courses for hard of hearing adults were much more unusual, possibly because some hard of hearing students with good English are able to integrate more easily with courses taught in English, especially if there is support. Lipreading classes specifically for adults who are hard of hearing were the commonest form of discrete provision. The Birmingham Resource Centre for Deafened People runs relaxation classes for hard of hearing adults and Bristol University Department of Continuing Education runs a range of leisure classes specifically for hard of hearing adults. Wood and Kyle (1993) report how often hard of hearing people feel excluded from adult education.

'It's a joy to be where people speak clearly and carefully, not too quickly, lots of written material and notetakers and a lipspeaker. What a pleasure to be able to go at your own pace' (hard of hearing student at Bristol University Department of Continuing Education).

Discrete courses for hard of hearing people require:

- a notetaker
- a lipspeaker
- tutors who are trained in clear speaking and hearing tactics
- rules of communication, such as taking turns and raising hands before speaking
- a loop system
- rooms with carpets, curtains and soft furnishings to absorb background noises so that they do not interfere with communication
- well-lit rooms so that people's faces can be seen clearly when they speak.

Integrated courses

There are many integrated programmes, with most of the work of Deaf or Hearing Impaired Support Units and specialist posts supporting students in integrated settings. The keys to successful integrated provision are well-planned and co-ordinated courses, suitable communication and interpreting for deaf and hard of hearing adults, coupled with suitable learning support, such as additional tutorials, literacy support, adapted printed material, etc.

TEC-supported integrated courses

North London TEC funds a four-day-a-week integrated business studies course with a fifth specialist support day each week for the deaf or hard of hearing students to provide leaning support appropriate to each learner and to cover all the extra issues that can crop up for the deaf or hard of hearing students. The support tutor for the deaf and hard of hearing students and sometimes the communication support worker may spend a great deal of time outside contact hours adapting material, reading information beforehand, as well as explaining work to students outside the class.

Combining integrated with discrete provision

Newham Community College provides both discrete and integrated courses. Deaf people can apply to any course and if accepted they may be supported by a communicator, a support tutor (teacher of the Deaf) or an interpreter. Sometimes courses may have a deaf tutor. Discrete provision includes adult basic education, written English and lipreading for students whose home language is neither British Sign Language nor English, British Sign Language, art and a conversation group for deaf and hard of hearing young people. There are 45 deaf people enrolled on general college courses who receive communication support. The discrete and integrated provision for deaf and hard of hearing adults is co-ordinated across the college by a support tutor (hearing) who works in the disability and learning support unit. The provision for deaf and hard of hearing adults operates within the framework of a strong college commitment to equal opportunities and an emphasis on opportunities for adults with disabilities and for people with learning difficulties.

Ingredients cited by the staff there as essential for success include:

- a policy and management commitment to provide both discrete and integrated programmes for deaf and hard of hearing adults
- resources allocated for this area of work
- specialist staff in the cross-college disability and learning support service with knowledge of deaf and hard of hearing issues and practical ways of ensuring needs are met
- a college emphasis on language development and communication, with many students who have English as second, third or fourth language. 'This creates a positive ethos of recognition and value for different languages, making it comfortable for deaf people – it's not the student's fault if they don't understand English.'
- a guidance system which helps individuals participate in programmes which are most suited to their learning preferences and ambitions, and which helps individuals negotiate for the type of support and provision they need
- good in-college liaison and contacts in the community with deaf and hard of hearing agencies
- monitoring of the effectiveness of provision for deaf and hard of hearing adults and a commitment that results of monitoring will inform future work in this area.

Open and distance learning

Open and distance learning can offer deaf and hard of hearing students opportunities which are flexible and where they can work in their own style and at their own pace.

The interactive learning packages of print material or, increasingly, computer software packages and interactive video mean that courses can be accessible to deaf and hard of hearing adults. For most students (hearing, deaf or hard of hearing) it is essential that what is offered is supported in open and distance learning. Clearly the support needs to be tailored to the needs of individual students and so for deaf and hard of hearing students may include British Sign Language materials, presenting assignments on video using British Sign Language, tutorials with a lipspeaker or interpreter, etc. Open and distance learning is most suitable for deaf and hard of hearing adults whose preferred language is English.

Some 3.2 per cent of students at the National Extension College have a disability, but it is not known what proportion of these are deaf or hard of hearing. Some deaf or hard of hearing students have found using the NEC distance learning packages very positive.

The Open Learning project based at Filton College, Bristol is producing open learning materials in information technology and adult basic education for deaf adults based on existing packs.

The Open University has clear policies on equal opportunities and disabilities, and through specialist staff offers a range of practical support for students with disabilities, from central and regional offices. For example it provides interpreters or communicators as appropriate for tutorials and for summer schools, and arrangements can be made for assessments to be done using British Sign Language on video. The University has developed specialist modules on courses, for example issues in deafness and social work with deaf people, with some excellent learning materials, such as videos in British Sign Language and adapted units.

Where deaf and hard of hearing adults learn

As with adult learning for hearing people, deaf and hard of hearing adults learn in a range of different settings and across different sectors. The main sectors include:

- community and voluntary organisations
- local specialist deaf and hard of hearing agencies and centres
- local authority adult education or community education services
- further education colleges
- higher education institutions
- national specialist deaf and hard of hearing agencies
- the workplace and trade unions
- other statutory services, such as social services, health authorities, economic development services, TECs, etc.

In addition, many deaf and hard of hearing adults will be involved in informal learning where they are teaching themselves skills, for example computing or gardening using books, television, videos, experimentation, etc., or where they are learning from friends or family members.

The various sectors providing educational opportunities for deaf and hard of hearing adults have particular strengths in the kinds of learning opportunities they can offer, the kinds of support they can offer and in the accessibility and suitability of their premises and facilities. Although within each sector there are often significant variations in the quality and accessibility of services for deaf and hard of hearing adults, there are examples of good practice to be found in each sector. Not surprisingly, local and national specialist deaf and hard of hearing centres consistently cater effectively for deaf and hard of hearing adults, offering a range of learning opportunities, although these are usually uncertificated and at introductory or intermediate levels.

Community and voluntary organisations

General community and voluntary organisations are usually well-placed to be accessible geographically and may be less intimidating than formal educational institutions. Because they operate on a smaller scale they are usually friendly, informal and can provide a personalised service. In addition, deaf or hard of hearing adults may well know other people from their neighbourhood who are participating in classes, which can make learning more social and more supportive. Provision is likely to be introductory or intermediate, often with a mix of uncertificated and certificated courses and informal and more formal classes.

Resources are usually limited and centres may lack specialist equipment and may not have access to specialist staff such as interpreters.

Local specialist deaf and hard of hearing agencies and centres

There is a network of local specialist deaf and hard of hearing agencies and centres across the country. These Deaf clubs, institutes, centres and societies are usually part of the Deaf community and although some hard of hearing groups may meet there and use the facilities, they are rarely involved in the running of the centres. Deaf clubs have grown up as charities over 150 years or so, and range from tiny clubs like Llanberis in North Wales to enormous clubs like Glasgow. Many grew out of the missioners' movement ('Deaf Missions', which were dominated by the welfare and religious aspects of work with Deaf people and saw Deaf people on the whole as passive recipients of welfare), but are now usually independent organisations. The pattern of Deaf clubs, societies, etc. varies in each area, as does the extent to which they work with statutory agencies such as housing, social services and education, with some working in very close partnerships. These organisations have been almost without exception very fertile ground for Deaf-led adult education.

Cheshire Deaf Society

Cheshire Deaf Society offers adult basic education and computer classes using British Sign Language, and was the base for the highly successful health promotion Aids programme for Deaf people, 'Aids Ahead', funded by the BDA. The Society is planning to run a City and Guilds 7307 tutor training course for Deaf tutors. The Society also tries to support Deaf members who want to participate in adult learning centres in the surrounding rural areas and at the local further education college. The society is extending access to libraries through video telephones and information technology. There are Deaf tutors, organisers and managers, all with close involvement and understanding of the Deaf community.

Merseyside Centre for the Deaf

The centre has established a wide-ranging adult education programme in addition to housing various independent deaf ventures such as 'Silent Views', a Deaf video production company. The programme includes a City and Guilds hairdressing course for British Sign Language users with 12 students, run by two hearing and one deaf tutor. Placements are in hearing salons as well as the hairdressing salon run at the centre. There is a City and Guilds basic skills course and a City and Guilds video production course taught by deaf tutors. Durham University ran a British Sign language tutor training course there, and the centre also runs a communicators' course. The centre has close links with Liverpool Community College, Millbrook College and other centres.

A great strength of the local Deaf centres is their experience and understanding of Deaf issues and the Deaf community. A wide range of adult education programmes is run by these centres across the country and increasingly they are offering certificated courses and progression routes to more advanced education, training or employment. Some centres are beginning to cater now for hard of hearing adults as well as the Deaf community, and widening opportunities for them.

Local authority adult and community education services

The range and types of provision for deaf and hard of hearing adults vary in these services, but often they are able to draw on specialist support from within the local authority, for example Hearing Impairment Services or funding sources, which can facilitate the development of discrete provision. These services specialise in adult learning and have professional commitment to principles and practices which support deaf and hard of hearing adults' participation, for example learner-centred approaches, building on people's experience, providing learning support appropriate to individuals, part-time provision which fits in with adults' existing commitments such as caring for young children. Provision may be discrete or integrated, and ranges from social and informal through to certificated courses.

Provision in adult education

The City Lit Institute, London provides a wide range of adult education programmes and also has a specialist centre for Deaf People and Speech Therapy. This centre provides discrete courses and support for deaf and hard of hearing adults on integrated courses both within The City Lit and in over 20 further and higher education institutions across London. The centre runs a discrete 'new start' course for deaf people newly arrived in Britain which includes British Sign Language, English (both written and spoken), maths and computing. There is also a British Sign Language course for users of other sign languages and American Sign Language is taught as a foreign language. There is a sign language teacher training course.

The lipreading, speech and hearing therapy section runs lipreading courses and lipreading teacher training courses. A new course is planned for lipreading students for whom English is a second language. The only course in the country for hearing therapists is at The City Lit. It is a one-year, full-time course and usually has a number of hard of hearing and deaf students. There is also in-service training for hearing therapists (hearing therapy is a relatively new profession which started in 1978 within the National Health Service). Hearing therapists often work with education staff in lipreading, hearing tactics and communication skills. In The City Lit hearing therapists teach on Deaf awareness courses for staff and students.

Support for deaf and hard of hearing students on integrated courses covers a wide range of courses and deaf students have won awards such as the John Double prize for fibrous plastering, second prize in a masonry competition and in a national woodworking competition. The centre actively employs deaf and hard of hearing lecturers and had a deaf head of centre at one stage. There is a full-time sign language interpreter, as well as deaf counsellors and a social work post.

The specialist centre supports students, staff and institutions across London and is a greenhouse for new initiatives for work with deaf and hard of hearing students.

'I like coming here. You meet other Deaf people in the coffee bar, you find out what's going on. There's always something happening.'

Further education colleges

Further education colleges have much experience of working with young people and adults with learning difficulties and disabilities, including deaf and hard of hearing adults. They often have specialist support units and access to specialist facilities, equipment and staff, for example interpreters. They offer integrated courses and often discrete courses, too. A great strength is their experience and the range of work-related vocational and academic courses, especially those which are qualification bearing. There are usually good progression routes into employment and increasingly to higher education.

Provision in a further education college

Park Lane College, Leeds runs several discrete courses for deaf and hard of hearing adults, as well as offering opportunities for integration across college courses. There are specialist support services for deaf and hard of hearing students. The college has developed a cross-college strategy for providing opportunities for deaf and hard of hearing adults. A discrete part-time English course for hard of hearing adults leads to the RSA Communicative Use of English for the Hearing Impaired. Most of the students are profoundly deaf, but two are partially hearing. Students can join at any time of the year and there are social events, meals out, theatre visits and presentation evenings. The total communication method is used and the course is triple-staffed with a course tutor, support teacher of the deaf and a British Sign Language interpreter. There are also discrete typing and word processing courses for deaf students. There are full-time deaf students on mainstream courses, for example the BTEC National Diploma in Business and Finance, with a sign language interpreter for each student. The college has a text telephone so that students can telephone for information.

The central support unit provides:

- language and communication support
- support for learning through, for example, extra tutorials
- language and communication skills courses
- staff and student Deaf awareness training
- help with applying for funding for programmes and for deaf and hard of hearing students.

Higher education

Some departments of continuing education have developed discrete provision for deaf and hard of hearing adults, for example Bristol University, but in general deaf or hearing adults are integrated into mainstream degree courses in universities.

The kinds and levels of support for students vary, but often there are special central staff or units which can advise. Students are eligible for additional financial support on full-time courses to help fund interpreters or facilities and equipment which may be needed for the student to participate fully in the course. In addition, some higher education institutions offer specialist modules on deafness and deaf issues in some courses, which may be of interest to both hearing and deaf adults. Some institutions also conduct research into deafness and related issues, thereby raising the general level of awareness and creating a body of knowledgeable staff who can help make higher education provision more accessible to deaf and hard of hearing adults. Access to higher education is vital for deaf and hard of hearing adults to gain qualifications and entry to a range of professions.

Provision in higher education

The Centre for Deaf Studies at Bristol University carries out research and has a Deaf Students' Access initiative supporting deaf students in the University and providing courses for deaf students. It offers diplomas, postgraduate courses and interpreter training. Full language and communication support is provided for students. Rooms in halls of residence are being made more accessible, with text telephones and suitable fire alarms, etc.

The Deaf Studies Research Unit at Durham University has produced the British Sign Language/English Dictionary and it runs the British Sign Language Training Agency. It also provides a postgraduate diploma course and interpreter training. Reading University has also helped pioneer work with deaf and hard of hearing students in higher education through Bulmershe College. It has developed language and communication support for students, as well as discrete courses such as drama and information technology. Wolverhampton, Derby and Central Lancashire Universities are also involved.

National specialist deaf and hard of hearing agencies

These are mostly voluntary organisations and are active in promoting and sometimes providing adult learning. Many are campaigning organisations working to ensure that policy-makers and the public are better informed about the Deaf community and Deaf issues and that services properly meet the needs of deaf and hard of hearing adults, for example in education. Many are involved in joint initiatives, often innovative work, with other adult education providers such as local Deaf centres or colleges. They are well-placed as national organisations to disseminate good ideas and practice developed with and for deaf and hard of hearing adults, through conferences, publications, etc. The key national specialist deaf and hard of hearing agencies are listed in Appendix 2.

The workplace and trade unions

The workplace is an ideal context for offering training opportunities to deaf and hard of hearing employees which help them carry out their existing job effectively and keep them up to date with developments in their field, or prepare them for more responsible or different positions within employment. Membership of a trade union can lead to development within the context of active union membership as well as personal and skill development. Many training courses run by employers or trade unions can have direct benefit for other aspects of participants' lives, for example literacy schemes, health and safety or first aid courses all have immediate applications outside of the work or union context.

Access to training at work for deaf or hard of hearing adults varies, but it seems that participation is lower than amongst hearing adults. Some employers contacted as part of the NIACE survey were well-informed about deaf issues and keen to ensure that proper povision was made for their deaf and hard of hearing employees.

Learning at work

Rolls Royce plc has a loop system in the lecture room at its Derby training centre, and lecture notes are distributed prior to training sessions at the company's Anstey training centre in the West Midlands. Sign language interpreters are used in employee education sessions, for example explanation of the share scheme or pensions options. Contact is made with specialist agencies for information, advice and for setting up training courses, for example with the Royal School for the Deaf in Derby.

Marks and Spencer use sign language interpreters in training and are having their training videos subtitled in British Sign Language.

The Post Office has a range of initiatives to support deaf and hard of hearing employees at work and in staff training including:

- using the *Access to Training* pack produced by the Royal National Institute for Deaf People
- using distance learning material
- making a referral to the British School of Motoring Centre for Disability in London for a driver who was hard of hearing
- installing loop systems in training rooms
- supporting employees to learn sign language
- supporting deaf employees on written English courses at local colleges as a development initiative.

The GPO also featured in *See Hear* as part of the Royal National Institute for Deaf People's campaign aiming to raise awareness of deafness amongst employers.

The Trade Union Congress is working on a Deafness Policy Statement with detailed recommendations about the rights of deaf and hard of hearing employees. Several trade unions run Deaf awareness courses for their members and some publish information and awareness-raising articles and booklets.

Statutory services

Statutory services other than education also provide learning opportunities for deaf and hard of hearing adults, for example hearing therapists in the health service provide training in lipreading and hearing tactics. A whole range of employment-related training is run through TECs and local authority economic units.

Job clubs and centres

North Tyneside TEC funds supportive job centre services including job clubs for deaf people through, for example, an information pack in video format in British Sign Language. Communication and language support are offered for interview skills, as well as literacy and computer and office skills training for job applications. Recently a number of deaf workers have been made redundant who are not used to applying for jobs or taking up training courses. The deaf job club is focusing both on their needs so that they can re-enter the labour market, and on awareness-raising with employers so that they recognise the skills and the contributions that deaf and hard of hearing employees can make.

North London TEC has provided a range of services for deaf and hard of hearing adults including:

- a communicator at Enfield College
- support for six trainees to study for a National Vocational Qualification in Business Administration
- extra tutorial support for deaf and hard of hearing students on mainstream training courses
- communication and technological support for a deaf upholstering student now self-employed on the North London Enterprise Scheme
- fax machines for trainees
- support for students on work placements
- advertising through the Channel 4 text information service

- Deaf awareness training for employers.

Different providers have different strengths which can be used for educational programmes for deaf and hard of hearing adults. No one type of provider can meet the full range of educational needs and ambitions, therefore collaboration between providers and clear routes of progression to more advanced education, training or employment for deaf and hard of hearing students are particularly important.

Many providers have little in the way of experience or specialist knowledge of deaf issues and ways of providing good quality provision for deaf and hard of hearing adults. The various specialist Deaf units and centres (some developed from specialist services for schools) often provide essential back-up services and support for colleges and other providers, sometimes also providing direct services for students. The City Lit's Centre for Deaf People and Speech Therapy is an important specialist centre for adult education provision across the London area, as well as for deaf and hard of hearing students on The City Lit's own educational programmes. There are other key specialist centres in some parts of the country, and where they exist they often help bring about improved levels of provision for deaf and hard of hearing adults across sectors. In the Derby/Nottingham area the combination of the Royal School for the Deaf, an active Deaf community, committed local authorities, colleges, higher education institutions and employers has led to a relatively good range of provision in the region. There is a 'value-added' effect of different providers 'sparking off' more programmes and facilities for deaf and hard of hearing adults as they work together and draw on each others' experience, generating greater awareness and new ideas. The specialist centres tend to have an energising effect in their surrounding areas. In areas where there are no specialist centres provision tends to be at an earlier stage of development.

The Royal School for the Deaf has played a role both in direct provision and in collaborative work with other agencies in the Derby/Nottingham area. Similarly the specialist centre at Coventry Technical College has led to improved local provision for deaf and hard of hearing adults.

Specialist unit provision

The Education Communication Support Retraining Advice (EC-STRA) Service for Deaf People is based at Coventry Technical College and works across the colleges in Coventry and is the post-16 specialist unit for Coventry Local Education Authority. It aims to enable deaf people to have the same access as hearing people to education and training opportunities. Currently it also houses the Coventry and Warwickshire Interpreter Unit, funded by the local social services departments and the health authorities. The range of services ECSTRA provides includes:

- teaching and communication support for deaf trainees and students in further higher education institutions
- adult basic education and social skills
- communication courses
- lipreading and sign language classes
- in-service training for staff and outside agencies, including Deaf awareness courses
- City and Guilds 730 teaching skills for Deaf tutors of sign language
- a resource base for initiatives such as the Communicators' Network and the Midland Sign Language Tutors' Support Group and for the National Association for Tertiary Education and Deaf people (NATED)
- publishing newsletters, information packs, teaching materials.

The unit provides direct support to students and teaching staff, as well as providing training, and it serves as a focus for activity and initiatives for deaf and hard of hearing adults in the local area and the region.

Where there are specialist staff in an institution this leads to an improved range and quality of provision for deaf and hard of hearing students within the institution and often helps stimulate developments in neighbouring centres. Clearly the impact one post can make is less than that of a specialist unit, and if it is a generic 'special needs' or equal opportunities post rather than a focused one for deaf and hard of hearing adults, the impact is diluted further because of all the other interests covered by the postholder.

Specialist part-time staff such as deaf subject tutors, lipreading tutors and interpreters can make invaluable contributions to work with deaf and hearing impaired adults and bring significant benefits to individual students. However, unless there is some kind of specialist co-ordinating post, institutional change and the development of a cross-institution strategy for work with deaf and hard of hearing adults is extremely unlikely.

Conclusion

Providers need to consider the benefits of discrete and integrated provision, of English or British Sign Language as the main language for teaching, of specialist posts and units and of the particular roles and contributions different types of providers can make in order to organise the best quality, most accessible and relevant learning opportunities for deaf and hard of hearing adults.

7

Staff Development and Training

Language and communication training
General communication guidelines

There are many different kinds of staff development opportunities for tutors and other staff working with deaf and hard of hearing adults. They fall into the following categories:

- language and communication training
- British Sign Language
- lipreading
- hearing tactics
- language and communication support
- Deaf studies
- Deaf awareness training.

Some courses are specifically designed as staff development opportunities, and some are general courses which staff may join for their own professional development alongside other students who are doing the course for different reasons. Staff development may be specifically for adult tutors or for a whole range of staff with different roles and working in different employment sectors.

Language and communication training

British Sign Language

Increasing numbers of people, both deaf and hearing, are taking up British Sign Language classes, which have been a tremendous growth area in adult education in the past few years. Hearing people have become much more aware of sign language through its increased use on television and in public services and events. Most adult learners in British Sign Language classes are hearing people. Participants have different reasons for wanting to learn British Sign Language, ranging from personal and social reasons – 'so I can communicate with my child, who is deaf'; 'so I can sign a bit with my neighbour, who uses sign language' – through to job-related reasons. For example:

- various professionals working with deaf people – social workers, police, nurses, teachers, research workers who want to be able to communicate with deaf clients
- those wanting to become British Sign Language interpreters as a profession.

Deaf tutors are increasingly becoming tutors for British Sign Language classes and for them teaching experience is often a staff development opportunity in itself, especially when teaching is combined with taking up tutor training courses such as the City and Guilds 730 'Helping Adults Learn' course.

> 'In 1974 I began teaching sign language only because I was dropped in it by the Missioner at the Centre for the Deaf. We'd invited a hearing youth club to come and play us at skittles. They were all interested in sign language and the Missioner asked me to teach them. That's how I got started. Now things have changed. There are so many British Sign Language classes! Sometimes there are 48 people in the room who have come to learn sign language' (Deaf tutor who also teaches a City and Guilds 730).

This tutor also points out the dangers of inexperienced and untrained tutors teaching British Sign Language:

> 'They go out and find anyone to teach the British Sign Language class – anyone Deaf will do! Are you doing anything Monday night? If not, they grab them to come in and teach. This is not fair to the Deaf person teaching or the students.'

In this tutor's view all those teaching British Sign Language should have the City and Guilds 730 qualification or equivalent.

Other professionals in a range of areas may decide to learn British Sign Language for varying reasons:

> 'I feel useless when someone gets brought into the hospital who is deaf. I can't communicate with them at all. Writing things down can be difficult, so I thought I'd learn some sign language' (a nurse).

> 'I want to be able to communicate better with the kids in my class' (a teacher in a school for deaf children).

> 'We have to complete stage 2 of the Council for the Advancement of Communication with Deaf People British Sign Language

classes before we're allowed to take on a post. Only one of our staff is deaf, a deaconess who is profoundly deaf and uses British Sign Language, the other 24 staff are mostly hearing, with a few who are hard of hearing' (a full-time Chaplain for the Ministry to Deaf People of the Church of England).

'I am a tutor working in adult education in Staffordshire. I hold the City and Guilds 730. I go to British Sign Language classes so that I will be able to reach deaf people who might come to adult education classes' (a partially deaf adult tutor).

'I thought to myself, this is my language, why should I watch hearing people get certificates in sign language? I want to do that too, to add it to my qualifications and maybe use it for work in the future.'

For those who want to teach British Sign Language there are routes through:

- the Council for the Advancement of Communication with Deaf People (CACDP) examinations; or in Scotland the Scottish Association of Sign Language Interpreters (SASLI)
- the Durham University British Sign Language tutor training course
- specialist British Sign Language tutor training courses offering the City and Guilds 730 qualification
- The City Lit sign language teacher training course.

There are three levels of qualifications through the Council for the Advancement of Communication with Deaf People – Stage One, Basic; Stage Two, Intermediate; Stage Three, Advanced – which all British Sign Language interpreters must pass. The examinations cover practical interpreting skills, test the level and range of British Sign Language a candidate has and include issues such as ethics and professional codes for interpreting. In Scotland SASLI offers training and qualifications at different levels for interpreting and registration for qualified interpreters.

The British Sign Language Tutor course at Durham University began in 1985. Some 169 people have now gained certificates from this course. It aims to provide training in tutoring British Sign Language. The course lasts 25 weeks and is part-time, including three one-week residential schools, a 10-week teaching placement of two hours a week and a range of distance learning options. The course was begun because the British Deaf Association's research on sign language in 1982 found that it was taught mainly by hearing people, and that the sign language taught was not proper British Sign Language, but more loke sign-supported English. The course set out to recruit deaf people using British Sign Language and was designed accordingly. Applicants are interviewed in British Sign Language, all of the teaching is done by deaf tutors, distance learning packages use home study video materials and assessments are made using sign language recorded on video.

> *'This tutor training course has given the Deaf community a sense of pride in their own language, which in the past has been mainly a matter of shame ... and their weakness (lack of competence in English) ... Many for the first time have shown their true potential (having previously been denied the opportunity to do so). It has enhanced their employment and training opportunities' (Clark Denmark, one of the original tutors on the 1990 OU course).*

Many of the deaf students on the course are sign language tutors in Local Education Authority adult education services and have been funded by their Authorities to do the course as a staff development opportunity.

Discussions are underway to establish a National Vocational Qualification for the sign language component of Durham University's British Sign Language tutor course and to extend it on a regional basis. Merseyside Centre for the Deaf played host to a course from Durham University, and other colleges are interested.

Several specialist City and Guilds 730 Further and Adult Education Teachers' Certificates for British Sign Language users and tutors have been run, for example at Hull College and the Cheshire Deaf Society. The City and Guilds 730 courses are in two stages, both are part-time and are usually generic, that is courses cater for tutors of different subjects. From September 1993 there has been a new competence-based 7305 which will make the accreditation of prior learning possible and include different forms of assessment. This may make the City and Guilds 730 course more accessible to deaf tutors if it relies less on written English. There is some discussion about whether generic City and Guilds 730 courses include enough of the specific issues and skills relating to teaching sign language, which is partly why several subject-specific British Sign Language City and Guilds 730 courses have been set up. There is a debate about the advantages and disadvantages of discrete and integrated City and Guilds 730 courses and the Durham University British Sign Language tutor training course and which of these is best for British Sign Language tutors.

Which tutor training course for British Sign Language tutors: views from participants

DISCRETE AND INTEGRATED CITY AND GUILDS 730 COURSE

'We should be the same as hearing people. I don't want a City and Guilds 730 (deaf) because people will think it's of a lower standard.'

'I don't want to go and do a 730 with hearing people. Why? Because I know I will find it difficult. I can understand with an interpreter, but it would be even better with a deaf tutor, easier and it saves money.'

'I learn a lot from being with hearing students, jargon especially. Hearing students can learn a lot from deaf students too. They become more aware.' (City and Guilds 730 students)

'I'm doing the course with an interpreter, funded by the Local Authority. I've learned a lot on the course about teaching a group, for example different ways of getting a group to stop chatting, such as asking one of them a question instead of telling them to shut up ... I wanted the same qualification as hearing people and I find I've learned from hearing people. I learnt how to change a nappy from a nurse when she did her practical teaching session, and I gave a case history to illustrate interpreters for mine. I gave the example of a deaf woman living alone who had no contact with the Deaf community and who only had a neighbour to go with her when she went to the doctor. The neighbour did a sort of lipspeaking for her, but when they were at the doctor's the neighbour got very involved in the conversation and forgot the patient. This illustration helped other students understand what interpreting was all about and how important it is to do it properly. My own interpreter on the 730 course is very good. She tells me everything that goes on throughout the time. I videoed some of my project. I realise that it is not my English that they are interested in, but the quality of information I am giving. I am very pleased with this new way of doing it and I hope it will work out' (a City and Guilds 730 student who had previously done the tutor training course at Durham University).

DURHAM UNIVERSITY BRITISH SIGN LANGUAGE TUTOR TRAINING COURSE

'The course is great. I enjoyed doing it, but the 730 helps you to teach anything, whereas this concentrates only on British Sign Language. I'm lucky to have done both.'

'I preferred the Durham University course to the 730. I understood everything that was going on. I learned about my language, about modulation, negation, the language in depth really. I think the Durham course is more important really. I felt lost going on the 730 after that.' (Tutors who had done both the City and Guilds and the Durham University British Sign Language tutor training course.)

The following list contains a number of suggestions for improving the City and Guilds 730 courses to make them more suitable for British Sign Language tutors, based on the experiences of deaf tutors going on these courses:

- an information pack about the course before it starts
- interpreters need to be knowledgeable about adult tutoring and the different subjects taught by tutors on the course
- continuity of interpreters, ideally the same interpreter employed throughout the course
- notetakers are needed as well as interpreters, as taking notes is impossible whilst watching an interpreter
- more use of graphics to aid communication on the course
- videos of lectures in sign language to take home and use for reference
- tutors should have had Deaf awareness training, as should other students on the course
- deaf tutors
- deaf moderators
- a choice of integrated 730 courses or separate ones for deaf tutors
- if sign language tutors are on 730 courses there should be some sign language subject input as part of the course, or as a supplement
- better access to information and publicity for potential deaf tutors who want to teach or are teaching British Sign Language or other subjects.

Some of these recommendation were made by graduates of the Hull 730 course for deaf tutors.

One City and Guilds 730 deaf tutor who used to teach forestry and then went on a City and Guilds course could not pay for an interpreter. He struggled to get through the course and lipread everything. He translated the course content into British Sign Language and made the whole course more visual. He has taught deaf people who teach underwater diving, women's health, sign language and finance and there are other deaf tutors running ABE, computing, drama and video courses. He feels that deaf tutors need something extra in their training but not necessarily a 'special' deaf course.

Another approach has been explored at Bradford and Ilkley College's Adult Education Department, which has run a pre-730 discrete foundation course for deaf tutors. The course runs for half a day a week over 12 weeks and has enabled students to gain the skills and confidence to go on to an integrated City and Guilds 730 course. Many of the participants on the foundation course were British Sign Language tutors or hoping to become tutors. The course was funded partly because of the lack of qualified sign language tutors.

A Training the Trainers Course has been proposed at Durham University for deaf tutors running City and Guilds 730 and other training courses.

Lipreading training

Participants in lipreading classes are generally people who have lost their hearing as adults and whose first language is English. Lipreading classes are essential for people who have lost their hearing to learn a new communication skill which will be used in personal, social and work contexts.

> *'I couldn't make sense of all these talking heads around me when I lost my hearing. I'd given up mixing with people, even at work. Now I find it possible to make some sense of what is going on, I don't have to be left out and I can join in more. The lipreading classes got me going again.'*

Some 80 per cent of the 450 lipreading classes offered nationally are run by adult education services.

Teachers of lipreading are usually working part-time, are often hard of hearing themselves and have limited access to training. Many lipreading tutors start teaching because of their own experience of losing their hearing: 'I am a lipreading teacher because I am hard of hearing myself and I know how important it is to feel confident and learn a new communication skill after your hearing goes.' Currently there are 194 members of the Association of Teachers of Lipreading for Adults (ATLA) but there are only two tutor training courses for lipreading tutors, one at The City Lit in London and one at Manchester Metropolitan University.

ATLA publishes a journal, *Catchword*, which provides a network for an otherwise rather isolated group of teachers. Some lipreading teachers are also lipspeakers. The Association of Lipspeakers provides support for lipspeakers, partly through its newsletter. Currently there are 50 members of the Lipspeakers Association. Staff development and support is limited both for lipreading tutors and for lipspeakers, depending in the main on special initiatives and networks between tutors.

Training lipreading tutors

In Norfolk, Local Education Authority officers wanted to run lipreading classes but could not find a qualified lipreading teacher. There was a strong demand for classes. Norfolk County Council and the British Association of the Hard of Hearing agreed to jointly-fund two lipreading teachers to attend the City Lit course. An advertisement was placed in the newspaper. Fifty people responded, 15 were interviewed and two applicants were selected. It cost £1,500 per person, one-third of which was for fees and the rest for travel, accommodation and subsistence. The tutors found the course very valuable and came back with a shopping list of what should be provided for lipreading classes: loop systems, carpeted rooms, soft lighting, etc. The tutors had also addressed issues such as publicising lipreading classes on the training course and they advised the Local Education Authority on what to include in publicity, the kind of language to use and where to put publicity. The two trained tutors came back not only qualified to teach but also aware of how to set up and run all aspects of the lipreading courses. They enthused many local heads of adult education centres and set up and ran four classes in the first year, which soon developed into seven classes running regularly, and more could be run if additional funding was available. There was no problem recruiting students: they were inundated with people who wanted to learn lipreading.

The Local Education Authority found working with the British Association of the Hard of Hearing (now called Hearing Concern) helpful, and although ATLA's role was small it was critical, and helped in the link with The City Lit and through membership of the National Institute of Adult Continuing Education, as well as advising on all stages of the plans for training lipreading tutors and setting up the lipreading classes.

Issues raised by this training for lipreading tutors included:

- should lipreading tutors need to do the City and Guilds 730 as well as the City Lit training course?
- some centre heads were not convinced of the need for funding lipreading tutors, although some were very enthusiastic
- initially the Authority and centre staff knew little about lipreading but learned through this initiative. Greater awareness of the importance of lipreading classes amongst hearing people in decision-making positions is important
- the importance of liaising with specialist hard of hearing organisations and specialist staff such as those at The City Lit
- the usefulness of gaining local newspaper coverage for the tutors when they qualified and for the lipreading classes, both for recruitment and raising public awareness.

Hearing tactics

Hearing tactics include communication skills for people who have lost their hearing and also basic skills for hearing people to aid communication with someone who is deaf or hard of hearing. Many staff development and Deaf awareness courses include some exploration of hearing tactics, with, for example, case studies of different workplace settings to show how staff with a hearing loss and their hearing colleagues could manage communication and work tasks. Hearing tactics courses are seen by some as rehabilitation and by others as education. Most participants on hearing tactics programmes are older adults who have lost their hearing in adult life and need to develop strategies for coping and communicating effectively in personal, family, social and work settings. Some courses also involve partners and families or work colleagues.

Tutors on hearing tactics programmes are mainly hearing therapists and lipreading tutors. Many are hard of hearing themselves. Some in-service training for tutors is available, for example the Birmingham Resource Centre runs training courses for staff working in health and social services. Hearing therapists' professional training includes hearing tactics.

Adult education providers may want to develop hearing tactics courses, or to build hearing tactics into other courses such as lipreading classes. Hearing tactics courses could be offered as in-service staff development to other services such as the police, and to private employers as well as to individuals. A lot can be gained from hard of hearing or deafened adults exchanging experiences and tips for avoiding miscommunication and confusion in discussion, and from sharing strategies for hearing and communicating well. Course organisers would find the involvement of hearing therapists or qualified lipreading tutors helpful for planning a course and setting it up. There are some useful published resource materials, and also centres with experience in this area, for example the Continuing Education Department at Bristol University, which runs courses on 'Living with a hearing loss'.

Hearing tactics courses may need training and support. The City and Guilds 730 is a useful general tutor training course, but specialist advice and information on hearing tactics may also be needed, drawing on various specialist agencies or staff.

Language and communication support

Chapter 3 described the different courses for British Sign Language interpreter training and communication training. These courses offer important staff training opportunities and a career route for deaf, hard of hearing and hearing people wanting to work with deaf and hard of hearing people by providing interpreting and communication support.

Deaf studies

Deaf studies is a relatively new area of work, mostly developed in universities and often linked with professional studies courses such as interpreter training courses. The Universities of Bristol and Durham have pioneered work on Deaf studies and more recently the University of Wolverhampton, the University of Central Lancashire at Preston and Derby University have set up Deaf studies courses or degree modules on sign language, deaf cultures and communication.

Deaf awareness training

There are now a number of Deaf awareness training courses available, which usually include:

- introduction to and awareness of British Sign Language
- Deaf culture and the Deaf community

- differences amongst deaf people
- basic communication skills.

Deaf awareness courses vary in length and are frequently provided for staff development purposes, especially for public services such as education, social services, the police, etc.

They are very useful for adult education staff who may have deaf or hard of hearing adults in their classes or wanting to join their classes in future. Courses are mostly taught or co-taught by deaf or hard of hearing tutors. The main aims of Deaf awareness courses are to help people understand more about being deaf or hard of hearing and give some basic skills in communication. They often provide powerful learning experiences for participants who may not have known much about deafness and deaf issues beforehand.

'It really made me think, hearing about their experiences'
(participant on Deaf awareness course in Norfolk).

Deaf awareness course run by Norfolk adult basic education services

A one-day workshop on Deaf awareness was run by the Norfolk adult basic education services. Evaluation sheets from participants reported that the most successful part of the day was having a panel of deaf and hard of hearing people who used a range of different languages and communication methods. The panel comprised:

- a deaf British Sign Language tutor using British Sign Language as well as speech
- a deaf British Sign Language tutor who did not use speech
- a hard of hearing lecturer from adult education who used a hearing aid and a loop system
- a deaf student who used British Sign Language
- a deaf literacy tutor who used British Sign Language and speech.

The panel members described their experiences of teaching and studying. One of the panel brought and used a portable loop system, demonstrating to participants how easy it was to set up and how relatively cheap it was. They could also see the effect it had for the hard of hearing speaker. Her face immediately lit up when it was switched on and she was able to follow the conversation. However, there was a danger of the loop seeming a complete and easy solution.

'You could see how relieved the participants looked when they thought the loop was all that was needed. You could see them thinking, oh is that all? Then I watched their faces as they saw the sign language communicator not using the loop and we were all watching her and understanding the signing, which they didn't understand all.'

Many of the participants saw an interpreter and heard English translations of inputs in British Sign Language for the first time. Participants gradually became aware of the complex issues involved, as well as the range of communication methods.

Deaf awareness and strategies

A Deaf awareness in-service day was run for tutors at Somerset College of Arts and Technology by Somerset Local Education Authority's tutor for the hearing impaired, who is partially deaf and communicated by speech and by lipreading. The day was packed with information and tutored with great energy and enthusiasm. The topics covered were:

- what is deafness, its causes and its effects on people
- methods of communication
- the Deaf community
- teaching strategies
- sign language interpreters and notetakers in classrooms
- language development and making language more accessible to deaf people
- support services and hearing aids
- the opportunity to try out various aids
- using videos
- exams and assessment.

The tutoring methods were inputs, experiential exercises, group discussions and feedback. There were regular breaks so that deaf and hard of hearing tutors on the course could go out and have a break for five minutes.

The participants were tutors in different subjects areas and each considered issues of working with deaf students in their own subject. For example, an art and design tutor who had recently started to wear a hearing aid himself felt that art and design was a good subject for deaf people because it is visual. Further, he felt that there was less discrimination because people are judged on artistic talent rather than oral or written communication. However, there were particular challenges for an art and design tutor working with deaf or hearing impaired students, including:

- art classes are usually held in large, echoing, rooms with high ceilings and no carpets
- some of the processes are noisy, which causes problems for hearing aid users
- students may want to listen to advice whilst actually doing some work, which is not possible for deaf or hard of hearing students who lipread or use an interpreter
- showing slides in the dark make it impossible to lipread.

The participants on the Deaf awareness course were enthused by the course, as this selection from their comments shows:

- enjoying lipreading exercises, which showed how easy it was to confuse words, for example 'bar snacks' and 'darts match'
- hearing about the teacher's own experiences as well as the masses of information he gave us
- how useful the teaching strategies part had been, including simple issues to bear in mind such as a noisy overhead projector making it impossible to hear for someone using a hearing aid, the usefulness of echoing techniques, where the tutor repeats questions from the group for the benefit of deaf or hard of hearing students, the importance of deaf or hard of hearing students sitting at the front and side of a teaching room so that they can see the tutor and other group members, no tapping on a microphone, which is agony for a hearing aid wearer, a discreet nod to students to show when to put on the radio microphone
- how useful it was to learn about equipment and practise using it
- valuing the chance to discuss how to find the right balance between meeting the needs of deaf and hard of hearing students in the group and the rest of the group, and pacing learning appropriately for all of them
- looking at the benefits of having deaf students; for example it encourages the tutor to prepare lesson plans and handouts
- learning simple ways to communicate, such as putting your fingers in the shape of a C to ask if a deaf student wants coffee, as well as ways of using support workers

- learning about published resources, such as Deaf awareness packs from various national agencies.

Deaf awareness courses for adult tutors, managers and other staff can make a great difference to the ways in which deaf or hard of hearing adults will be received and supported by institutions and in mainstream classes. In addition to participating in staff training events such as Deaf awareness courses, a lot will also be learned by working and learning alongside deaf or hard of hearing people in the everyday life of the institution. For example, a hearing worker who shared an office with a deaf colleague did not realise that everytime the phone rang, she went to answer it when they were in the middle of a conversation. His experience, because he had not heard the phone ring, was that their conversation was suspended with no explanation, which was very irritating. Daily contact and discussion about aspects of communication that might be annoying or difficult can help change and improve the nature of communication. Deaf awareness courses are an important first stage, and can be built on through the experience of working with deaf and hard of hearing adults.

General communication guidelines

This chapter on staff development concludes with a guide to the essential points for hearing people to bear in mind when communicating with deaf or hard of hearing people.

Key issues in communication in learning and learning support are also listed.

General communication guidelines for hearing people meeting deaf or hard of hearing people

Find out how the other person wants to communicate first.

Always make sure that you have their attention first, without coming up behind them and startling them.

Look straight at the other person and keep looking!

Don't cover your mouth with your hands, smoke, drink a cup of coffee or eat whilst talking.

Make sure there is as little noise in the background as possible if the other person uses a hearing aid.

Talk at normal speed, slightly slower but not exaggerated and distorted, which makes it difficult to lipread.

Don't stand with the light behind you (against a window, for example), as it is hard to lipread a face in shadow.

Do not shout. It is quite pointless to someone who is profoundly deaf and it distorts speech patterns for someone who is trying to lipread. It also hurts the ears if someone is wearing a hearing aid.

If something is not understood, change the words used.

Always put the context first before going into detail. Don't say 'Oh, it was awful this morning, it was pouring with rain, it took me hours to get here, the car broke down', leaving the deaf or hard of hearing person wondering what the topic is. Say 'My car broke down', then the details.

Be expressive, use gesture and body language.

Make contact by showing in your face rather than by your tone of voice how you feel about the subject under discussion.

If all else fails, write things down.

Key notes for tutors/lecturers

The main thing is to remember that fluster and complexity do not help. Students who are deaf or hard of hearing will be quite used to trying to understand hearing people who do not know how to communicate with them, so they will have had plenty of practice with people like you. The fact that you are willing to learn is a good start!

First of all, is the student using sign language by following an interpreter? Or is s/he using English by wearing a hearing aid and the loop system, or trying to lipread what you are saying (with or without a hearing aid) or following a notetaker?

The distinction between the two is important and different approaches are needed for:

- people who are deaf and use sign language
- people who are deaf or hard of hearing and use English.

Key issues for working with people who are deaf and use sign language and for using a sign language interpreter

1. Ask the student where they want to sit in order to follow.

2. Try and meet the deaf person and the interpreter or notetaker beforehand to sort out communication and run through materials, such as a video.

3. Watch your language. Double meanings can be incomprehensible in sign language; for example, 'to carry out' can mean to do or to physically carry out; 'take steps to' can mean to set in motion, to walk or a process.

4. Always relate to the deaf student, not the interpreter, as your main relationship is tutor to this student. The 'does he take sugar?' syndrome makes people feel humiliated or awkward. Always look at them and maintain eye contact with them, not the interpreter (apart from hello, goodbye and thank you!) during work-time. The interpreter is there for the benefit of you and the student. Communication between you would not be possible at such a high level without the interpreter. You both need the interpreter.

5. Make sure that the rest of the group know how to communicate with the deaf student by:

- Deaf awareness training within your group, institution or region
- asking the deaf student to explain to the group some basic rules of communication which would help them
- attending sign language classes if they are interested.

6. Always give written material to the student and the interpreter beforehand.

7. Make sure members of the group always raise a hand when they want to say something so that the deaf person knows who is speaking.

8. Don't speak at the same time that overheads are on. Allow time to read material, as it is impossible to watch a notetaker/interpreter and read at the same time.

9. Don't ramble on, going off at tangents: keep sentences clear and short.

10. Check whether deaf students need additional tutorial time to go over things. Liaise with the supported learning team if there is one.

11. Do not adopt a slower pace unless the interpreter asks you to. Always allow the interpreter to finish before moving on. A deaf person watches the question from the interpreter, then might turn around to raise their hand but can find the group has moved on unless sufficient time is allowed.

12. Do not mind being asked to slow down or repeat things!

Key issues if a student is hard of hearing/deafened and using a hearing aid with the loop system and/or notetaker or following a lipspeaker

1. Ask the student where they want to sit and check that the loop is working (if relevant). Discuss with them the best way to organise communication.

2. The same communication rules apply: raising hands before speaking and not putting up overheads whilst talking.

3. Slow the pace down (not too much). Keep things clear and structured, and do not mind when you are asked to slow down.

4. Provide written material wherever possible. Make sure it is available beforehand where possible for lipspeakers, notetakers and the students. Prepare handouts on the topic as well as the structure of a lecture or seminar. These will make it much easier for someone trying to lipread.

5. Keep down background noise: students clattering out of a room next-door or the noise of traffic through an open window can drown any attempts to hear through a hearing aid. Thick curtains, carpets, etc. help to muffle background noise, so if possible use rooms with soft furnishings.

6. Face the student if they are lipreading you and remember not to turn and write on a flipchart whilst talking. Do not have your back to the window, as this makes it hard to see the face in detail.

7. Allow time for breaks, as lipreading is very tiring.

8. Speak clearly, in a structured way, with no or few asides and speak at a slower pace.

It is important that other key people are also aware of these guidelines, for example:

- non-teaching staff such as reception staff, canteen staff, etc.
- other students
- employers taking students on placement
- examiners, assessors, etc.
- deaf and hard of hearing students themselves.

Sometimes it is assumed that deaf and hearing impaired students are aware of all these issues, but it could be that they have never worked with an interpreter before or may not have used a loop system. It is important to make sure that the student knows the communication arrangements planned for them and that they feel comfortable with the approaches to be used and any special equipment or facilities.

A combination of curriculum development and effective approaches to teaching and learning strategies can quite quickly make an enormous improvement to the educational opportunities available for deaf and hard of hearing adults.

8

Funding, Management and Policy Issues

Sources of funding

Management and policy issues

Providing learning opportunities for adults who are deaf or hard of hearing poses challenging questions for providers:

- how to provide learning opportunities for deaf and hard of hearing adults which are of the highest quality
- how to overcome feeling intimidated into inaction by the exacting challenges of work in this area when funding and resource levels seem inadequate
- how to determine what it is possible to do to improve learning opportunities and language and communication support for deaf and hard of hearing adults, whilst still aspiring to higher standards and increased opportunities.

Despite constraints, there are examples of individual courses, departments or institutions achieving successful participation of and outcomes for deaf and hard of hearing adult learners across the country. Characteristically, these have employed a holistic approach to provision and have included:

- staff informing themselves about deaf issues, deaf and hard of hearing adults, differences between deaf people and the various specialist agencies or support units which can be drawn upon
- identifying needs and involving deaf and hard of hearing adults in the planning of provision
- providing guidance
- setting up discrete and integrated opportunities, often on an outreach basis accessible to deaf and hard of hearing people
- ensuring that suitable language and communication support is offered by using human aids to communication such as interpreters or notetakers and technological aids such as a loop system or a radio microphone

- identifying and attracting funding for the programme and for students from internal and external sources and by drawing on contributions in kind, tailoring programmes according to resources available
- working closely with a number of different agencies to help with various aspects of provision; for example publicity, negotiating with examination bodies for assessments to be suitable for deaf and hard of hearing adults, making sure there is progression for participants, etc.

Putting together all the elements for a course for deaf or hard of hearing adults, or providing suitable language and communication support for deaf or hard of hearing adults to participate in other courses is often like trying to complete a complicated jigsaw where the pieces have first to be found and key pieces are often missing.

Combining resources

'We have to try creative accounting. We had a young woman with funding for full-time communication support to do an NVQ in Business Administration Level 2. We also had a woman in her thirties who had tried and failed to do a course elsewhere as the local TEC would only fund five hours a week for communication support. A man, also in his thirties, had tried a computer adult training course, but with an interpreter for only one day out of five. They had both dropped out. It was a waste of money not to give enough support like that ... what we did was we infilled these two students into the Business Administration course where there was full-time communication support for the young woman student, and they could have a weekly two-hour tutorial with communication support too. Everyone wants to fund young people; they are just not interested in older people. It's going to be terrible to find funding for older deaf students from now on' (a lecturer in adult education in the North of England).

'We have managed to get money from the local TEC towards our school leavers course. It is the old City and Guilds Diploma in Vocational Education. We use it as a framework really for all sorts of learning for older students' (a lecturer from the Midlands).

Providers often spend considerable time identifying and then harnessing expertise and resources in order to mount programmes. A combination of resources which has been carefully constructed and is effective for one programme is not readily transferable to other programmes, or even available another time to run the same programme again. Provision for deaf and hard of hearing adults is frequently made vulnerable because of the changing priorities of funding agencies and the short-term nature of their pump-priming or development funding. It is usually difficult to secure mainstream or permanent funding even after pilot programmes have proved themselves. Securing funding takes up considerable amounts of managers' time.

Effective provision for deaf and hard of hearing adults can be expensive because there are additional elements which need to be built into programmes: more face to face publicity approaches requiring more staff time, recruiting and supporting suitable new staff, adapting materials and assessment procedures, and of course providing and monitoring language and communication support. However, some elements needed for programmes can be cheap and immediately make a significant difference to accessibility and quality for deaf and hard of hearing adult learners. For example the installation of a loop system can be fairly low cost and can make it possible for new hard of hearing students to join classes timetabled in that room; it can also reduce drop-out of existing students who may be hard of hearing. Similarly, training and using notetakers can be relatively inexpensive yet make an enormous difference to deaf and hard of hearing adult learners.

Sources of funding and other resources

There are several different key sources of funding, and these funders are often major providers of other kinds of resources and support for programmes for deaf and hard of hearing adults. The main ones include:

The Further Education Funding Council (FEFC)

The Further Education Funding Councils for England and for Wales are the major sources of funding for further education curriculum areas for adults which were listed in Schedule Two of the Further and Higher Education Act 1992:

- vocational and academic qualification-bearing courses which include all the major awarding bodies' qualifications such as NVQs,

GCSEs, A-levels, BTEC, Pitman, RSA and City and Guilds Qualifications, etc.
- access to higher education courses
- courses which lead to any of the above
- basic literacy and numeracy courses
- English literacy and numeracy courses
- independent living and communication skills for adults with learning difficulties which lead to any of the above
- Welsh language for adults in Wales.

Providers mounting discrete or integrated provision in any of these
curriculum areas for deaf and hard of hearing adults can seek to secure
funding for them from the FEFCs. Further education colleges, sixth form
colleges, the Workers' Educational Association and a few named institutions such as the adult residential colleges can receive funding directly
from the FEFC. Other agencies or institutions offering provision which
falls into the Schedule Two categories can receive FEFC funding only via
one of the directly funded institutions. Providers should contact their local
FEFC-funded institutions to discuss possibilities for funding.

The Further and Higher Education Act's broad definition of 'learning
difficulties' includes those who by reason of a physical disability, sensory
impairment or learning difficulty are not able to study at the level 'you
would expect for their age'. Adults who are deaf or hard of hearing may
be classified as having 'learning difficulties' as defined by the Act.

The Further Education Funding Councils are developing funding mech-
anisms which will provide funding for programmes (including pre-entry,
on programme and exit elements) which institutions have a duty to provide.
In addition, funding will be allocated to individual students assessed to
have learning difficulties. These two funding methods mean that providers
are able to resource discrete provision by combining programme and
student linked funding, as well as fund support as required for individual
students with learning difficulties to infill onto any other courses. The
funding mechanism's flexibility makes it suitable for provision for deaf
and hard of hearing adults wanting to study any Schedule Two course.
However, there is concern that the unit of resource may be driven down
in order to maximise student numbers. Low units of resource may mean,
for example, large numbers of students in classes, which can militate
against their accessibility for deaf and hard of hearing adults.

The Further Education Funding Council has set aside funding specifically for students with disabilities and learning difficulties (some seven
million pounds for 1993/4) and has set up a committee to focus on the

needs of students with disabilities or learning difficulties. Specialist staff have been appointed to support and develop provision for students with disabilities and learning difficulties.

Many institutions directly funded by the FEFC, for example further education colleges, have specialist staff or units for students with 'special needs' which can include deaf or hard of hearing adults and in some cases posts or units specifically for deaf and hard of hearing students. These units and staff are a valuable source of information, advice and support within the institution. They also may be able to contribute time and resources (if not funding as such) to help others who offer Schedule Two provision for adults who are deaf or hard of hearing on a partnership, or possibly a more formal, contractual basis.

Local Education Authorities

Local Education Authorities have a duty to provide educational opportunities for adults which fall outside the courses listed in Schedule Two of the Further and Higher Education Act. Local Authorities receive funding for this provision from central government through the Revenue Support Grant. Each Local Education Authority can determine its own priorities for funding for adult education, and indeed whether they enhance the level of funding (or in some cases choose to reduce it) from their own internal budgets. Many Local Education Authorities earmark funding for special needs adult education provision from within their total adult education budget.

Local Education Authorities usually fund and run their own adult education services (sometimes through a specialist adult education service or a differently focused service such as leisure services). They frequently also fund adult education providers in the voluntary sector.

In any locality the Local Education Authority is likely to be the major funder, or contributor of resources and expertise, for adult education provision for deaf and hard of hearing adults which lies outside the Schedule Two list.

In addition, many Local Education Authorities, mainly because of their statutory responsibility for school-age children, have set up specialist units such as hearing impaired support services. These services have in many cases provided support for further and adult education sectors. There is serious concern that central services like these are being lost because funding for further education colleges, sixth form colleges and some adult education provision has been moved from the Local Education Authority to the Further Education Funding Council, and because school budgets are increasingly being devolved to schools from the Local Education Authority. Consequently a much smaller amount of funding is held centrally by the Local Education Authority, making funding central services or staff of any kind difficult. In theory schools and even further education colleges or sixth form colleges could buy in services from a specialist central Local Education Authority service such as a hearing impaired support service. The fees paid could then help core-fund the service. In practice this arrangement for central units can prove difficult because of the unpredictability of income from sales. Those Local Education Authorities which had specialist further education deaf and hard of hearing staff or units are discontinuing them after 1993, except possibly in a much slimmed-down form to support non-Schedule Two courses for deaf and hard of hearing adults.

Although Local Education Authorities may no longer be able to offer as much specialist central support for institutions wanting to develop provision for deaf and hard of hearing adults, they continue to have a number of useful sources of funding or support which can include:

- development funding or grants for providers to offer courses for specific target groups of adults such as deaf or hard of hearing adults
- fee remission schemes for adults from certain groups such as those who are unemployed. In some cases deaf or hard of hearing adults may qualify for remission
- discretionary grants for students
- a bank of support equipment such as portable loop systems, overhead projectors, etc.

Other Local Authority services

Social services departments may provide some social or personal support for individuals who are deaf or hard of hearing, for example help with transport. They also may help contribute to programmes for deaf or hard of hearing adults, particularly when they relate to their areas of responsibility, such as parenting skills or child development courses. They may help with publicising opportunities amongst deaf or hard of hearing clients, and may refer clients.

Other Local Authority departments such as leisure, tourism, libraries, museums and economic development units may all be able to contribute either funding or support through their service specialist, for example an economic development unit may help fund or even fully fund a training programme designed for deaf or hard of hearing adults to enter employment, or it may fund individuals to go on a training course. The library service may agree to purchase suitable videos or books to support a course which is being set up for deaf or hard of hearing students and house them in the library based nearest to the course location so that students may have easy access to them.

Health authorities

Specialist staff such as audiologists or hearing therapists may assist with designing programmes and publicising them. They may also be able to contribute to teaching, for example on lipreading or hearing tactics courses. North Derbyshire Health Authority hearing therapists run lipreading and relaxation classes.

Health promotion services may also contribute expertise or staffing, and some also run valuable initiatives for deaf or hard of hearing adults, for example the Health Promotion Authority of Wales, which has worked with the Aids Ahead awareness-raising and educational programme for deaf adults.

Training and Enterprise Councils (TECs)

TECs focus on economic development and employment, aiming to secure economic stability, growth and a suitably skilled workforce in their local area. They fund major training schemes for unemployed people, and aim to increase the attainment of National Vocational Qualifications in schemes they fund and those funded by others. Many TECs have specialist staff with a brief for special needs which will include deaf and hard of hearing adults. Funding is mainly allocated to the major employment and youth training schemes, but TECs also have some development and local initiatives funds which providers may be able to secure for work-related programmes for deaf and hard of hearing adults. The level of provision and support for opportunities for deaf and hard of hearing adults varies between TECs. Some TECs have developed excellent work for deaf and hard of hearing adults, and have funded communication support for groups or individuals.

TEC initiatives for deaf and hard of hearing adults

Suffolk TEC funds a Teleworking project for deaf people in floristry which provides on-site training combined with supported distance learning using text telephones and fax machines in people's homes which the TEC has provided. North Tyneside TEC funds a supportive Job Centre which provides video information about the Centre's range of services in sign language, as well as literacy and skills training for job applications followed by the provision of communication support for job interviews, for example a sign language interpreter.

Voluntary organisations

Specialist national voluntary organisations for deaf people sometimes have funding for supporting local initiatives, often those of an innovatory or developmental nature. Both national and local specialist voluntary organisations can contribute considerable expertise and knowledge at all stages of programme development, from initial needs identification, publicity and programme planning through to final evaluations. They can advise and help with finding tutors and deaf or hard of hearing students. (See Appendix 2 for a list of the main specialist voluntary organisations.)

Specialist centres for deaf and hard of hearing students

Support services and units for deaf and hard of hearing adults in educational institutions similarly have much expertise and knowledge and can advise on different aspects of educational opportunities for adults.

Higher education

Several universities have specialist research centres and provision for deaf and hard of hearing adults, notably the Universities of Durham, Bristol, Reading, Wolverhampton, Central Lancashire and Derby. Staff working in this area may be able to contribute to course planning. Departments of Continuing Education may be interested in setting up jointly funded and run initiatives, especially those relating to higher education programmes which could offer university accreditation.

Employers

Employers may help with publicising opportunities for deaf and hard of hearing adults. Employers may also contribute to programmes, for example by providing work placements or shadowing opportunities. They may also contribute to the design of return to work programmes, especially if the course may train deaf and hard of hearing adults for jobs in their companies. Both private and public sector employers may contribute in these ways. Local Authorities are usually major employers in their local areas.

Charities and trusts

A number of charitable trusts may be approached for funds for provision for deaf and hard of hearing adults, and for funding for individual students. Many companies also have trust funds with an educational or training emphasis.

Central government

A number of central government departments have funds for supporting local initiatives or pilot programmes of national significance which may be suitable for supporting educational programmes for deaf and hard of hearing adults. One example is City Challenge funding to selected urban areas, which focuses on the regeneration of the economic and social infrastructure of an area and can be used to fund training programmes, new training centres, etc. Local Authorities bid for City Challenge funding on a competitive basis after drawing up a comprehensive regenerative strategy for a chosen urban area within their boundaries. Providers need to work with the Local Authority and build provision for deaf and hard of hearing adults into the overall plans submitted to central government.

European funding

European funding has been used at Bradford and Ilkley College to fund a youth work training programme, at Merseyside Centre for the Deaf and at the Cheshire Society for the Deaf to fund adult learning programmes. This is a fast-growing area of funding, but it is short-term and insecure.

Broadcasting

Much broadcasting, both programmes specifically for deaf and hard of hearing people and general programmes, has enormous educational value and can be used to provide a sound resource base for learning opportunities for deaf and hard of hearing adults.

Distance learning providers

Distance learning materials can be a valuable resource for courses for deaf and hard of hearing adults. Distance learning materials can also be used to complement taught courses. The Open University has specialist staff and facilities for deaf and hard of hearing students and may be able to advise on using Open University course materials with deaf and hard of hearing adults. Their Community Education materials may be appropriate for a wide range of adult education courses for deaf and hard of hearing adults.

Management and policy issues

Working collaboratively with different agencies for funding purposes and to enhance other aspects of provision is often essential in order to set up and run provision for deaf and hard of hearing adults which a single provider could not do alone. Collaboration can contribute significantly to improving the quality of existing provision. However, collaboration with other agencies raises a number of issues for management to address:

- which agencies are most suitable to work with for any particular initiative
- how best can the agencies work together
- what skills or specialists do each of the agencies bring and how can these best be harnessed
- what are the ground rules for collaboration
- how will decisions be made
- who 'owns' the initiative
- how will the different partners be accountable to each other
- what organisational information is shared, and what might be considered confidential
- how can joint working be participatory and use time efficiently
- who initiates and who concludes collaborative work and how are these phases managed
- how can collaboration be focused, purposeful and lead efficiently to practical benefits for deaf and hard of hearing adult learners.

The NIACE survey (see Appendix 1) showed that educational provision for deaf and hard of hearing adults is generally underdeveloped in England and Wales, despite the existence of successful, but fairly isolated, examples of good practice. There are important management and policy implications which derive from both the general lack of suitable provision for deaf and hard of hearing adults and as a result of lessons learned from successes in this kind of provision.

Management and policy issues and recommendations are wide- ranging and are touched upon in all of the earlier chapters. The following range of management and policy issues attempts to focus on selected key elements. Readers are advised to refer to other chapters for more details.

Access and progression

Fundamental questions for managers to address are who participates in provision and, conversely, which groups do not participate and may be excluded? The NIACE survey showed that existing discrete provision for those with a hearing loss was almost entirely for deaf adults who use British Sign Language. There was very little evidence of provision specifically for deafened or hard of hearing adults or for deaf and hard of hearing adults who may have a disability, for example deaf-blind adults, or for those who have a learning difficulty. Many of the providers surveyed felt they had developed provision for deaf and hard of hearing adults because they run British Sign Language classes. However, analysis of who takes up British Sign Language classes shows that in fact most participants are hearing. Providing British Sign Language classes does not ensure participation of deaf and hard of hearing adults, neither do these classes necessarily bring any indirect educational benefits to deaf or hard of hearing adults. Managers and policy-makers need to consider:

- do deaf and hard of hearing adults participate?
- if so, which groups of deaf or hard of hearing adults participate, for example men/women, different black and other ethnic or linguistic minority communities, different age-groups, those who have had least educational benefit in the past, those with disabilities or learning difficulties, deaf or hard of hearing adults with different communication needs?
- which groups of deaf and hard of hearing adults do not participate and how could they be reached in future?
- how are admissions processes arranged so that they are suitable for deaf and hard of hearing adults?
- how is student participation monitored so that there is a clear picture of who participates and in which programme areas?
- how can the participation rates for deaf and hard of hearing adults be increased across programme areas?

Some deaf and hard of hearing adults participating in learning opportunities will aim to progress to more advanced education or training, to go into work, to gain promotion in work, or to become more involved in a voluntary or personal capacity in the community. Some deaf or hard of hearing adults will want to participate in learning opportunities for their own sake. It is important that progression is made possible for those who want to move on to other opportunities. Access to accreditation may be very important for some deaf or hard of hearing adults, including access to accreditation through different routes, for example the accreditation of prior learning.

Managers and policy-makers need to consider:

- how to ensure that there are clear progression routes to other education, training or employment opportunities
- the need for some targeted provision which focuses on progression, for example preparation for work courses or Access to higher education courses. Progression-led courses may be either specifically for deaf or hard of hearing adults or be part of provision designed also for hearing adults
- how progression is monitored.

Needs identification

There is a danger that some deaf or hard of hearing adults are so used to their educational needs or interests not being met that they do not actively articulate their needs to providers. This is more likely to be true for hard of hearing adults or adults who have a disability or learning difficulty in addition to being deaf. Deaf adults who use British Sign Language are more likely to identify their needs and articulate them, and to do this collectively from within the Deaf community. Providers need to identify the educational needs and interests of both deaf and hard of hearing adults, and to be sensitive to those hard of hearing adults who feel that they have little or no purchase on educational provision. Creative means of needs identification may be required to reach a broad cross-section of deaf and hard of hearing adults. Finding out what people want is important so that provision and language and communication support can be tailored to meet needs. Maintaining provision on a speculative basis for deaf and hard of hearing adults is highly risky and is not recommended.

Managers and policy-makers need to consider:

- the best ways of finding out what kinds of provision deaf and hard of hearing adults may want, for example visits to Deaf clubs (with a Deaf facilitator and interpreter if hearing staff go), finding out from any deaf or hard of hearing staff, finding out from any existing deaf or hard of hearing students, etc.
- how to ensure contact is made with deaf and hard of hearing adults from different backgrounds, for example black or other ethnic or linguistic minority groups, gay or lesbian groups, older and younger people, etc. to avoid a focus on a narrow group of deaf or hard of hearing adults

- how to collaborate with other agencies in order to identify needs, for example local or national specialist deaf or hard of hearing organisations (See Appendix 2 for information about key specialist organisations), or specialist staff in other services such as audiologists in the health service, social workers for the deaf, etc.
- ways of prioritising educational needs identified and then setting up programmes or language and communication support for mainstream provision to meet needs.

Curriculum

The NIACE survey showed that there was usually a very narrow range of discrete provision for deaf or hard of hearing adults, focusing mainly on adult basic education and information technology for deaf people using British Sign Language, lipreading for older hard of hearing adults and British Sign Language, mainly attended by hearing adults. It is important that deaf and hard of hearing adults have access to as wide curriculum range as hearing adults do.

Managers and policy-makers need to consider:

- how to extend the curriculum offer for deaf and hard of hearing adults so that it mirrors the range available to hearing people, offering choice, accreditation and progression
- how to improve the range of discrete courses for deaf and hard of hearing adults, and language and communication support facilities for deaf and hard of hearing adults so that they can participate in all other provision
- deciding on which language will be used for teaching any new programmes, for example sign language, Gujarati, English
- monitoring take-up of provision and effectiveness of communications support offered.

Guidance

Many deaf and hard of hearing adults may have had little benefit from education in the past and may see educational opportunities as being for adults for hearing people rather than for them. Therefore information about the range of courses available and the chance to discuss which learning opportunities may be most suitable is especially important for deaf and hard of hearing adults. In order for guidance to be accessible for deaf and hard of hearing adults, it needs to be available with communication support.

Managers and policy-makers need to consider:

- how to offer guidance with appropriate communication support such as sign interpreters for deaf people and notetakers for hard of hearing adults wanting to take up some kind of learning opportunity
- how to ensure guidance is available before entry to a programme, during the course and at exit so that the deaf or hard of hearing adult learner is able to make informed choices at each stage
- ways for guidance to raise deaf and hard of hearing people's interest in education and their ambitions.

Publicity

Information and publicity needs to reach deaf and hard of hearing adults so that they are aware of both discrete opportunities for them and the ways in which mainstream provision can cater for their particular needs by offering communication support.

Managers and policy-makers need to consider:

- including in printed publicity details of discrete provision for deaf and hard of hearing adults and details of communication support available for deaf and hard of hearing adults for these and other programmes
- using different approaches to publicity such as open days with interpreters specifically for deaf and hard of hearing adults in educational establishments, in community settings and in specialist organisations such as centres for deaf people; seeking referrals through specialist services for deaf and hard of hearing people; making a video prospectus using sign language
- conveying clearly in any kind of publicity a commitment to providing opportunities for deaf and hard of hearing adults
- monitoring the effectiveness of different publicity approaches.

Communication and learning support for deaf and hard of hearing students

Deaf and hard of hearing adults use many different approaches to communication. The language and communication support offered needs to reflect the diversity of approaches used, for example notetaking, British Sign Language, using a loop system. Communication support should be available across all curriculum areas, and most importantly should be in response to the preferred method of communication for each student. Discrete provision for deaf adults where the teaching and learning language medium is British Sign Language may need to include communication support, such as interpreting or lipspeaking for deaf or hard of hearing adults who may want to join the course and use English. Although providing suitable language and communication support to meet each individual student's needs may sound complex and almost impossible to achieve, in practice it is often possible to find some method(s) in common amongst a student group. A significant improvement to the accessibility of learning opportunities can be made through simple, low-cost strategies, for example tutors providing a printed general course outline, followed by printed notes for each session of the programme (which of course can be extremely helpful for hearing students too), increasing the use of visual aids in teaching, training and supporting volunteer notetakers, etc.

Managers and policy-makers need to consider:

- how individual deaf or hard of hearing adults' preferred methods of communication are identified
- what is the current range of communication support available and how this can be extended if necessary
- how the availability of communication support is conveyed to deaf and hard of hearing students and potential students
- how tutoring staff are informed about the range of communication support for deaf and hard of hearing students and potential students
- how tutoring staff are informed about the range of communication support they can draw on for deaf or hard of hearing adults on their courses
- monitoring the effectiveness of language and communication support taken up, and in particular getting feedback from deaf and hard of hearing students who have used support facilities.

Deaf or hard of hearing adults may be unfamiliar with formal education or training and the different approaches to teaching and learning now used. Deaf adults who use British Sign Language may be unfamiliar with learning alongside hearing people, especially if they went to a Deaf school. Many deaf or hard of hearing adults may not have had the chance to learn using different kinds of communication support and may need help to maximise the usefulness of support provided.

Managers and policy-makers need to consider:

- how to inform deaf and hard of hearing adults about the kinds of teaching and learning methods which will be used on courses
- preparing guidelines and information sheets for deaf adults who join classes with hearing people on strategies for learning alongside

hearing people and learning through using different kinds of communications support such as working with an interpreter, how to use a loop system, etc.

Consultation and participation in decision-making

The importance of finding out what deaf and hard of hearing adults' educational needs and interests are and responding to them has already been established. The subsequent process of negotiation about the kind of provision which can be set up to meet these needs can be done through consultation or participation, or by a combination of both. Essentially, consultation is when the provider designs the provision (ideally informed by needs identified) and then seeks the views of deaf and hard of hearing adults with a view to modifying provision if needed. Participation means deaf or hard of hearing adults are involved in the actual design of provision at all stages. Often a combination of participation and consultation is used, with a few deaf or hard of hearing people involved in designing provision and then other deaf and hard of hearing adults being consulted.

Participation of deaf and hard of hearing adults and consultation with deaf and hard of hearing adults about provision makes high quality, popular programmes a much more likely outcome.

Managers and policy-makers need to consider:

- seeking advice and support from specialist deaf organisations on how to involve deaf and hard of hearing adults in decision-making processes
- how to involve deaf and hard of hearing adults in planning, setting up and evaluating programmes and communication support
- how to ensure effective participation of deaf and hard of hearing adults in decision-making relating to provision and support, for example by having fair ways of selecting those who participate, having clear ground rules about participation and clear roles for participants
- how to avoid pitfalls in involving deaf and hard of hearing adults, such as tokenistic involvement of one deaf person on a planning group, or making key decisions outside of the forum which involves deaf or hard of hearing adults. Viv Lindow (1992) produced a useful set of guidelines based on users' views of how not to involve a group of people in decision-making, and although she drew on the experiences of adults with mental illnesses, the guidelines are highly relevant for services for deaf and hard of hearing adults

- ways in which the different communication and learning needs of deaf and hard of hearing adults can be represented amongst those involved in decision-making about provision
- how to carry out effective consultation with the particular groups of deaf or hard of hearing adults for whom provision is designed, or a cross-section of deaf and hard of hearing adults for general provision
- how the views of deaf and hard of hearing people inform management's decision-making across the whole institution.

Self advocacy

Self and group advocacy is growing amongst the Deaf community in particular, although it is far less well developed amongst hard of hearing adults. In some cases deaf, or more commonly hard of hearing adults, may censor their own claims to publicly-funded provision on the assumption that educational provision is by definition not for them. Deaf and hard of hearing organisations play a key role as advocates and also in providing opportunities for deaf or hard of hearing people to develop the skills of self and group advocacy. Other providers can also encourage the development of self and group advocacy by seeking out views and welcoming approaches and requests from deaf and hard of hearing adults. It may also be useful to provide courses in self and group advocacy, possibly drawing on the experience of the Deaf Service Users Participation Project in Warwickshire, which piloted training courses for deaf people wanting to become involved in decision-making for service provision.

Managers and policy-makers need to consider:

- how they can support and encourage self and group advocacy amongst deaf and hard of hearing adults
- how they can best deal with requests made by deaf or hard of hearing individuals and groups in ways which show respect for their views and their right to express them, and show a willingness to respond, whilst sharing information about realistic constraints which may determine to what extent demands can be met
- how to ensure that the institution does not deter deaf or hard of hearing individuals and groups from expressing their views about provision.

Collaboration

The introductory section on management and policy issues explored some of the main aspects of collaboration. Collaboration with various agencies is often central to making possible provision for deaf and hard of hearing adults. It can lead to fruitful co-operation rather than potentially damaging competition, and to a coherent, planned range of provision for deaf and hard of hearing adults.

Managers and policy-makers need to consider:

- how to best collaborate with other agencies
- how to draw out the strengths and gains from collaboration and avoid damaging divisions and conflicts
- ways of monitoring the range, purposes and outcomes of collaboration.

Continuity of provision

Provision for deaf and hard of hearing adults is often short-term and episodic, involving different staff running different short-lived special courses. Although a fixed diet of provision is not ideal, far greater stability and continuity in provision is needed to ensure quality opportunities for deaf and hard of hearing adults.

Managers and policy-makers need to consider:

- how to attract more secure funding for provision for deaf and hard of hearing adults, making continuity of provision possible
- ways of providing stable staffing for guidance, admissions, teaching and communication support so that experience and expertise are built up, leading to working relationships with deaf and hard of hearing students which are more easily established and maintained (many deaf and hard of hearing students have found a changing communication support staff disruptive and particularly difficult to deal with)
- providing core courses for deaf and hard of hearing adults on a fairly permanent basis, with a complementary range of provision which may change more often depending on needs.

Staffing

Employing deaf and hard of hearing tutors and other staff can help significantly in offering suitable and accessible learning opportunities for deaf and hard of hearing adults. The lack of coherent training and recognition nationally for various communication support staff has led to a fragmented workforce in this area, with varied levels of skill and codes of practice. This does not seem to enhance or secure high quality and reliable communication support for deaf and hard of hearing adults.

Managers and policy-makers need to consider:

- ways of recruiting deaf and hard of hearing teaching and other staff across the institution for provision specifically for deaf or hard of hearing adults and across the range of other courses
- supporting the Commission of Enquiry into Human Aids to Communication's recommendations for systematic qualifications and professional registration for human aids to communication such as sign language interpreters, notetakers, interpreters for the deaf-blind, lipspeakers, etc., which would provide a framework for ensuring the creation of an identifiable national profession
- employing qualified interpreters and other communication support staff paid at the standard professional rate
- monitoring of employees so that management has information about staffing profiles, including those who are deaf or hard of hearing and those with communication skills relevant to working with deaf or hard of hearing adults.

There is growing support for an effective system of staffing which combines generalist and specialist staff. A suggested network of staff attached to a programme for deaf or hard of hearing adults would include three kinds of staffing:

1. generalist teaching staff with some knowledge and skills relating to provision for deaf and hard of hearing adults

2. staff with more developed awareness and skills for working with deaf and hard of hearing adults (similar to the model of barefoot community doctors in Tanzania)

3. highly trained, specialist professional staff for work with deaf or hard of hearing adults.

The generalist staff can draw on the skills of both the 'barefoot' staff and on specialist staff to ensure that provision and communication support is the most suitable and the of highest possible quality for deaf and hard of hearing adults. Some people only subscribe to such an arrangement as a transitional process until there are sufficient highly trained specialist professional staff available.

Managers and policy-makers need to consider:

- how to ensure that all teaching staff have some basic awareness and knowledge of working with deaf and hard of hearing adults and that they know how to draw on staff or services with more specialist knowledge
- employing 'barefoot' specialist staff and locating them in the most relevant parts of the organisation so that they can support teaching staff and contribute to, or even run, certain programmes for deaf and hard of hearing adults or provide communication support
- making sure that there is access to support and involvement of highly trained specialist professional staff, possibly through purchasing their services from a specialist unit as and when needed for provision or communication support.

Staff development

A range of staff development opportunities is needed so that teaching and other staff are aware of deaf issues and have knowledge and practical skills for working with deaf and hard of hearing adults.

Managers and policy-makers need to consider:

- offering Deaf awareness courses for all staff
- making sure that teaching staff can participate in City and Guilds 730 courses and other teacher training courses, either general or specifically for: deaf or hard of hearing tutors teaching across a range of curriculum areas; staff teaching on target provision for deaf or hard of hearing adults, for example lipreading tutors, Deaf studies tutors; British Sign Language tutors
- making sure that interpreters and communication support staff have access to suitable and nationally recognised training and qualifications
- providing introductory or foundation courses which prepare deaf or hard of hearing staff for further training, especially if subsequent training is with hearing staff enabling deaf or hard of hearing staff
- ways of allowing those working in deafness curriculum areas to move into other curriculum areas if they choose and building in suitable staff development opportunities so they can do this successfully
- ways of enabling deaf and hard of hearing staff to participate in general in-house or external staff development programmes such as short management courses or MBAs, etc.

- providing professional development courses for deaf or hard of hearing staff from a range of professions, for example accounting or social work
- monitoring staff development opportunities which support provision for deaf and hard of hearing adults and staff who are deaf or hard of hearing.

Specialist units

The Commission of Enquiry into Human Aids to Communication recommended that a network of regional communication support units for deaf or hard of hearing communications is established. For adult education, links with these proposed regional support units would be invaluable. However, the various specialist education support units which operate currently within Local Education Authorities, further education colleges, etc. are valuable centres of expertise which can help support provision and offer some communication facilities for deaf and hard of hearing adults. Ideally, they can give advice, loan technological equipment and provide specific learning, language and communication support where needed. They may also provide a greenhouse environment for developing and piloting new initiatives for deaf or hard of hearing adults and then subsequently support such initiatives in colleges, local centres, etc. Specialist centres can play a vital role in disseminating ideas, advice, information, innovative and good practice and key contacts for work with deaf and hard of hearing adults. In practice, existing specialist centres are unevenly distributed across the country and are rarely able to function in such a comprehensive way to support adult learning opportunities for deaf and hard of hearing adults.

Managers and policy-makers need to consider:

- supporting the Human Aids to Communication campaign which aims to gain support for a network of regional communication support units
- setting up or further developing existing specialist units so that they are more evenly distributed across the country and can offer a good range of support services for adult learning opportunities for deaf and hard of hearing adults
- how best to draw on any existing specialist units to support provision and communication
- the suitability of their network of support arrangements.

Planning, monitoring, reviewing and evaluation

These core general management functions are particularly important in relation to provision for deaf and hard of hearing adults. Without focused attention on provision, this area of work is likely to continue to be underdeveloped, and where it exists to be fairly invisible and marginal in the institution.

Managers and policy-makers need to consider:

- how to ensure that the institution as a whole includes in its planning, monitoring, reviewing and evaluation cycles a focus on provision for, and participation of deaf and hard of hearing adults
- monitoring of participation and progression of students, the provision offered and staffing relating to deaf and hard of hearing adults
- ways of involving deaf and hard of hearing adults in making decisions about information to be collected for monitoring purposes, and how to conduct monitoring exercises sensitively and effectively
- ways of involving deaf and hard of hearing students in review and evaluation processes
- how to use information collected through monitoring to guide future developments in provision.

Funding for provision

Programmes and communication support for deaf and hard of hearing adults are relatively expensive and are mainly funded on a short-term basis, often relying heavily on 'hidden' contributions of staff time. Charges for provision vary from free to full-cost fees. The Commission of Enquiry into Human Aids to Communication recommended ways of ensuring holistic provision for everyone who is deaf. This may not be possible immediately but is a goal to work towards.

Managers and policy-makers need to consider:

- how to secure longer-term permanent funding for discrete provision for deaf and hard of hearing adults and for communication support for integrated provision
- ensuring that realistic levels of funding are available to provide quality provision with sufficient communication support
- how to attract different sources of funding and combine these for opportunities for deaf and hard of hearing adults
- offering free or low-cost discrete provision, as many deaf or hard of hearing adults are unemployed or on low incomes

- including deaf or hard of hearing adults in fee remission schemes
- monitoring funding dedicated specifically for opportunities for deaf and hard of hearing adults, with a view to assessing whether further investment is needed.

Funding for deaf and hard of hearing students

The disabled students allowance needs to be extended for part-time students, rather than being available only for full-time students. This is especially important for deaf and hard of hearing adults, who often have a range of existing personal and work commitments and responsibilities preventing them from studying on a full-time basis. Without an allowance, studying part-time can be prohibitively expensive, especially if there is not adequate free communication support from the provider.

Managers and policy-makers need to consider:

- establishing a communication allowance payable to the student, which will provide continuity of support throughout a course
- identifying when programme-linked funding and when funding allocated directly to students is most beneficial for deaf and hard of hearing adults' learning.

Legislation

The legislative base for deaf and hard of hearing adults' participation in learning opportunities through the Further and Higher Education Act rests primarily on the duty to deliver adequate or sufficient levels of provision. Definitions of 'adequate' or 'sufficient' are determined by the main funders and providers, the Further Education Funding Councils and Local Education Authorities. There have not yet been test cases of failure to provide adequate or sufficient levels of provision.

A more robust legislative framework for educational provision for deaf and hard of hearing adults is needed to strengthen and extend the level and range of provision available. Other areas of legislation can also contribute significantly to improving opportunities, for example legislation for people with disabilities. In the USA, the People with Disabilities Act focuses on rights rather than needs for access to public and other services and opportunities.

In Sweden and in the European Community Parliament, British Sign Language is recognised as an official language. The recognition of sign language in Britain would alter the position for deaf people using British Sign Language by making interpreting and translation a basic right.

Policies

A number of different policy areas are relevant for ensuring that there are learning opportunities for adults who are deaf or hard of hearing, for example Equal Opportunities. Where policy specifically focuses on deaf or hard of hearing adults it provides a strong base for developments. For example Hammersmith and Fulham local authority has an Equality/Quality policy which specifies a commitment to funding language and communication support for hard of hearing adults to take up adult learning programmes and the need for appropriately presented information about the authority's services, such as a video for people with different disabilities. Central and local government policies and individual providers' policies can be drawn upon to support work with deaf and hard of hearing adults.

Managers and policy-makers need to consider:

- examining existing policies and ensuring that they are used to support provision for deaf and hard of hearing adults, including for example:
  - equal opportunities policies
  - special needs policies
  - staff development policies
  - employee development policies
  - the Commission of Enquiry into Human Aids to Communication policy recommendations on training, funding and provision of a whole range of human aids to communication
  - National Education and Training Targets
  - the TECs' Group 10 Special Needs Committee's policies
  - the Further Education Funding Councils' policies, etc.
- drawing up policy which specifically addresses educational opportunities for adults who are deaf or hard of hearing
- reviewing policies and their implementation to ensure that there is a direct relationship between policy and practice.

In an ageing society, with increasing numbers of adults who will have a significant hearing loss, policies on provision for adults who are deaf or hard of hearing are needed urgently to underpin work over future decades.

Planning

Strategic, development and business plans are increasingly used as management tools to help ensure that implementation of policy is carefully planned and put into effect.

Managers and policy-makers need to consider:

- drawing up specific planning strategies and documents for work with deaf and hard of hearing adults
- how to make sure that plans include targets which are realistic and specific so that they can be achieved, for example to offer four free discrete courses with 12 places each during the first year, to guarantee student entitlement to notetaking and use of a portable loop system for any curriculum area, etc.
- systematic review of plans to see if they have been met.

Conclusion

Deaf and hard of hearing adults' educational needs and interests can be met if there is suitable provision and communication support. However, this area of work is still relatively underdeveloped in Britain, although there is good practice to draw on. Initiatives which will make significant improvements in opportunities for deaf and hard of hearing adults also often bring about general improvements in the quality of provision for all adults. Managers and policy-makers play a vital role in ensuring that further developments for deaf and hard of hearing adults are firmly located in the fabric of the organisation. In turn, management and policy-making can benefit enormously from involving deaf and hard of hearing people as learners, teachers, managers and policy-makers.

References and Further Reading

Brennan, M., Colville, M. and Lawson, L. (1984) *Words in Hand*, Moray House.

Commission of Enquiry into Human Aids to Communication (1992) *Report*.

Conrad, R. (1979) *The Deaf School Child*, Harper and Row.

Corbett, J. and Barton, L. (1992) *A Struggle for Choice: Students wirh special needs in transition to adulthood*, Routledge.

Davis, A. (1987) 'Epidemiology of hearing disorders', in Stephens, D. *Adult Audiology*, Butterworth.

Faraday, S. and Harris, R. (1989) *Learning Support*, Skill/FEU/Training Agency.

Finkelstein, V. (1991) 'We are not disabled, you are', in Gregory and Hartley, *op. cit.*

Foster, S. and Walter, G. (1992) *Deaf Students in Post-Secondary Education,* Routledge.

Grant, B. (1990) *The Deaf Advance*, BDA.

Green, C. and Nickerson, W. (1992) *The Rise of the Communicator: A perspective on post-16 education and training for deaf people*, Moonshine Books.

Gregory, S. (1991) 'Deafness in fiction', in Gregory and Hartley, *op. cit.*

Gregory, S. and Hartley, G.M. (eds) (1991) *Constructing Deafness*, Frances Pinter Publishers/Open University.

Groce, N. (1985) *Everyone Here Spoke Sign Language. Hereditary deafness on Martha's Vineyard*, Harvard University Press.

Hevey, D. (1992) *The Creatures That Time Forgot*, Routledge.

Higgens, P. (1980) *Outsiders in a Hearing World. A sociology of deafness,* Sage Publications.

Holcomb, M. and Wood, S. (1992) *Deaf Women. A parade through the decades,* Dawn Sign Press.

Jackson, P. (1990) *Britain's Deaf Heritage*, Pentland Press.

Jones, L., Kyle, P. and Wood, P. (1987) *Words Apart: Losing your hearing as an adult,* Tavistock.

Jones, L. and Pullen, G. (1990) *Inside We Are All Equal. A social policy study of deaf people in the European Community,* Brussels: ECRS.

Jones, L. and Pullen, G. (1992) 'Cultural differences. Deaf and hearing reseachers working together', *Disabilty, Handicap and Society*, 7, 2.

Kyle, J. (1989) 'Some aspects of sign language/English interpreting', *Deafness*, 1, 5.

Kyle, J. and Woll, B. (1985) *Sign Language. The study of deaf people and their language,* Croom Helm.

Lane, Harlan (1984) *When the Mind Hears*, Random House.

Lindow, V. (1992) 'Just lip-service?', *Nursing Times*, 2 December.

McGivney, V. (1990) *Education's For Other People: Access to education for non-participant adults,* NIACE.

Miles, D. (1988) *British Sign Language: A beginner's guide,* BBC.

Nuru, N. (1993) 'Multi-cultural aspects of deafness', in Battle, D. (ed.) *Communication Disorders in Multi-cultural Populations*, Andover Medical Publishers.

OPCS (1988) *Survey of Disability*, HMSO.

Open University (1991) *Issues in Deafness: Unit 1, Perspectives on Deafness.*

Padden, C. and Humphries, T. (1988) *Deaf in America. Voices from a culture,* Harvard University Press.

Sacks, O. (1991) *Seeing Voices,* Picador.

Sainsbury, Sally (1986) *Deaf Worlds*, Routledge.

Sargant, N. (1991) *Learning and 'Leisure': A study of adult participation in learning and its policy implications*, NIACE.

Schulman, J.S. (1991) 'Hollywood speaks: deafness and the film entertainment industry', in Gregory and Hartley, *op. cit.*

Social Services Inspectorate (1990) *Signposts*, HMSO.

Sutcliffe, J. (1990) *Adults with Learning Difficulties: Education for choice and empowerment,* NIACE/Open University Press.

Taylor, G. and Bishop, J. (eds) (1991) *Being Deaf: The experience of deafness,* Frances Pinter Publishers/Open University.

Woll, B., Kyle, J. and Deuchar, M. (1981) *Perspectives on British Sign Language and Deafness*, Croom Helm.

Wood, P. and Kyle, J. (1993) *Hearing-Less Instruction: Adult education and acquired hearing loss,* University of Bristol, Centre for Deaf Studies.

Wooley, M. (1981) 'Deafness', in Campling, J. (ed.) *Images of Disability*, Routledge.

Wooley, M. (1987) 'Acquired hearing loss, acquired oppression', in Kyle, J. (ed.) *Acquired Hearing Loss, an International Conference,* Clevedon: Multi Lingual Matters.

Appendix 1

NIACE Survey of Educational Provision for Deaf or Hard of Hearing Adults

Information on how people who are deaf and hard of hearing are participating in adult learning was collected between 1991 and 1993 by a postal survey across England and Wales sent to:

- Colleges of Further Education
- Institutes of Adult Education
- Local Education Authorities
- Workers' Educational Association
- Polytechnics (now Universities)
- University Departments of Continuing Education
- Training and Enterprise Councils
- Open College Networks
- Voluntary Organisations
- Social Services
- Health Authorities
- Centres and societies for the Deaf
- Trade Unions.
- 200 of the largest business contacts on the NIACE employer database

The survey was also advertised in relevant journals. There were some 950 replies in total, some from individuals as well as from organisations. Information requested included:

- any details of innovative work with deaf and hard of hearing people
- local contacts with whom any work had been done
- details of equal opportunities or special needs policies relating to deaf and hard of hearing people.

Appendix 2

Key organisations

Deaf

BDA (British Deaf
Association)
38 Victoria Square
CARLISLE
CA1 1H
Tel: 0228 48844

NADP (National
Association of
Deafened People)
c/o Geoffrey Brown
103 Heath Road
WIDNES
WA8 NU7

NDCS (National Deaf
Children's Society)
24 Wakefield Road
LEEDS
LS26 OSF

National Union of
Deaf People
c/o BDA
38 Victoria Square
CARLISLE
CA1 1H

Royal Association of
the Deaf
27 Old Oak Road
LONDON W3 7HN
Tel: 081 743 6187

RNID (Royal National
Institute for Deaf
People)
105 Gower Street
LONDON WCIE 6AH
Tel: 071 387 8033

Hard of Hearing

Hearing Concern
7–11 Armstrong Road
LONDON W3 7JL
Tel: 081 7431110

Multi-sensory

National Deaf Blind
Helpers League
18 Rainbow Court
Paston Ridings
PETERBOROUGH
PE4 6UP
Tel: 0733 73511

SENSE
The Deaf Blind and
Rubella Association
311 Gray's Inn Road
LONDON WC1X 8PT
Tel: 071 278 1005

Regional Associations for the Deaf

Midland Regional
Association for the
Deaf
75 Midhurst Road
King's Norton
BIRMINGHAM
B30 3RA
Tel: 021 458 4557

North Regional
Association for the
Deaf
144 London Road
Northwhich
CHESHIRE
CH9 SHH
Tel: 0606 330362

South East Regional
Association for the
Deaf
c/o Whitethorns
Rannoch Road
Crowborough
EAST SUSSEX
TN6 1RA

Wales Council for the
Deaf
Maritime Offices
Woodland Terrace
Maesycoed
Pontypridd
MID-GLAMORGAN
CF37 1DZ
Tel: 0443 485687
Minicom 0443 485686

West Regional
Association for the
Deaf
Centre for the Deaf
17 St Mary's Square
GLOUCESTER
GL1 2QT
Tel: 0425 20747

Sign Language Interpreters

CACDP (Council for the Advancement of Communication with Deaf People)
Pelaw House
School of Education
University of Durham
Leazes Road
DURHAM
DH1 1TA
Tel: 091 374 3607

Lipspeakers/ Lipreading

Association of Lip Speakers
P Bennett
7 Sparkbridge Road
HARROW
Middlesex
HA1 1TJ

Association of Teachers of Lip Reading to Adults
Mrs Rae Davies
7 Camelot Close
Orchard Glad
HEREFORD
HR4 9XH

Communicators/ Communication Support Workers

NATED (National Association for Tertiary Education and Deaf People)
c/o Parkwood Tertiary College
Shirecliffe Road
SHEFFIELD
S5 8XZ

OR

Chris Green
BTEC Consortium
University of Derby
Deaf Studies
DERBY

Other Organisations

ADSUP
Alliance of Deaf Service Users and Providers
c/o Hollybush House
Bondgate
NUNEATON
CV11 4AR
Tel: 0203 327667 (voice)
0203 327110 (text)

BACOD
(Sympathetic Hearing Scheme)
Breakthrough Trust
Charles Gillett Centre
998 Bristol Road
Sellyoak
BIRMINGHAM
B29 6E

British Society of Hearing Therapists
Hearing Therapy Department
Leicester Royal Infirmary
LEICESTER
LE1 5WU

British Tinnitus Association
Room 6
14–18 West Bar Green
SHEFFIELD
S12 DA

Communication Centre
East Court Mansion
Council Offices
College Lane
East Brinstead
SUSSEX
RH19 3LT
Tel: 0342 323444 (voice)
0342 312639 (text)

Communication for All: Human Aids to Communication Campaign
603 Charitybase
50 Westminster Bridge Road
LONDON SE17 QY
Tel: 071 7620 (voice)
071 7689 (voice & text)

Deaf Accord
(Policital Lobby Group)
Address as above

Deaf Broadcasting Council
c/o 592 Kenilworth Road
Balsall Common
COVENTRY
CV7 7DQ

Hearing Therapy
Association
The Link Centre for
Deafened People
19 Hatfield Road
EASTBOURNE
East Sussex
Tel: 0323 638230

London Deaf Access
Project
South Bank House
Black Prince Road
LONDON SE1 7S7
Tel: 071 587 0818

The Makaton
Vocabulary Project
31 Firwood Drive
CAMBERLEY
Surrey
GU15 3QD
Tel: 027 61390
(A language
programme for people
with learning
difficulties)

Ménière's Society
98 Maybury Road
WOKING
Surrey
GU21 5HX
Tel: 0483 740597

RNID Bucks
Interpreter and
Communication
Support Service
Walton House
Walton Street
AYLESBURY
HP21 7QQ
Tel: 0292 3922941
(voice)

Tel: 0296 392295 (text)

RNID East Sussex
Interpreter Unit
Warwick House
Warwick Road
SEAFORD
East Sussex
BN25 1RY
Tel: 0323 892484

RNID North Regional
Interpreter Unit
30 Broad Street
SALFORD
M6 5BY
Tel: 061 745 9128

RNID Wessex
Interpreter Unit
13B Church Farm
Business Park
Corston
BATH
Avon
BA2 9AP
Tel: 0225 874460

SHAPE
1 Thorpe Close
LONDON W10 5XL

National Subtitling
Library for Deaf People
Victoria Mill
STOCKPORT
SK8 5HN
Tel: 061 449 9650

Television Programmes

See Hear
BBC Television
Room 2319
White City
201 Wood Lane
LONDON W12 7PS

Sign On (including
Deaf World
Newswatch)
Tyne Tees TV Ltd
City Road
NEWCASTLE UPON
TYNE
NE1 2AL
Tel: 091 261 0181 ext
3173 (voice)
091 232 5523 (text)

Text Information Services

Chas Donaldson
Editor, *Read Hear*
PO Box 701
GLASGOW G42 AXG
Tel: 041 632 0024
(BBC Ceefax Teletext
magazine for deaf and
hard of hearing people)

Telecommunications and Technology

Teletec
Sunningdale House
49 Caldecote Lake
Drive
Caldecote Business
Park
MILTON KEYNES
MK17 8LF

Tel: 0908 270003
(produces Minicoms in
this country)

RNID Typetalk
Pauline Ashley House
Ravenside Retail Park
Speke Road
LIVERPOOL
L24 8QB
Tel: 051 494 1797
(voice)
051 494 1000 (text)

Wavelength BRECH
3 Windsor Square
Silver Street
READING
Berkshire
(Information service
for people with
disabilities)

Deaf-Fax Enterprise
Europe
Research and
Development Centre
on Deafness
University of Reading
Bulmershe Court
EARLEY
Reading RG6 1H7
Tel: 0734 351936

Video

Deaf Owl Productions
Redheugh Studio
Cuthbert St
GATESHEAD
Tyne and Wear
NE8 2HL
Tel: 091 477 9203
Fax: 091 490 1643

International Organisations

International
Federation of Hard of
Hearing People
Radegunder Strasse 10
A-805 Graz
Austria
Tel: 43-316671327
Fax: (43) 316681093

World Federation of
the Deaf
PO Box 65
SF00401 Helsinki
Finland
Tel: 3580 58031
Fax: 3580 5803770

European Regional
Secretariat of the Deaf
Rue Franklinstraat 110
B-1040 Brussels
Belgium
Tel: 02 7357218
Fax: 027 359354